Homeland and territorial security with AI

Aitek 6 knowledge cartridge

Bruno Ciroussel

COPERNICUS IP

Édition : BoD – Books on Demand, info@bod.fr
Impression : BoD – Books on Demand, In de
Tarpen 42, Norderstedt (Allemagne)
Impression à la demande
Dépôt légal : Avril 2024

Cover Graphics: Copernicus IP

All rights reserved for all countries. No part of this text may be reproduced in any form or by any means, electronic or mechanical, without the prior permission of the publisher.

First edition: June 2023

© 2023, Bruno Ciroussel

ISBN : 978-2-3225-2480-8

Copernicus IP

Rue Saint-Pierre 18

CH-1700 fribourg

Table of contents

LIMINARY 6
INTRODUCTION 8
   Chapter 0.0: reminder - the aitek platform 11
   Chapter 0.1: reminder: Knowledge Cartridge 32
PART 1: 39
   Chapter 1.0: homeland security concept 40
   Chapter 1.1: Homeland in Aitek: Approach 51
   Chapter 1.2: Homeland in Aitek : Model 57
   Chapter 1.3: Homeland in Aitek : BigData 70
   Chapter 1.4: Homeland in Aitek: Config 98
   Chapter 1.5: Homeland in Aitek: Admin 130
   Chapter 1.6: Homeland in Aitek: Supervisor 160
   Chapter 1.7: Homeland in Aitek: Performance 198
   Chapter 1.8: Homeland in Aitek: Dashboard 203
   Chapter 1.9: Homeland in Aitek: Supervisor Setup 207
   Chapter 1.10: Homeland Security + ... 222
   Chapter 1.11: Homeland Security ++ 229
PART 2: 235
   Chapter 2.0: Territorial Security Concept (Aitek) 236
   Chapter 2.1: Territorial Security Approch (Aitek) 241
   Chapter 2.2: Territorial Security & Beacon (Aitek) 244
   Chapter 2.3: Territorial Security & Architecture (Aitek) 252
PART 3: 257
   Chapter 3.0: Aitek Plateforme Setup 258
   Chapter 3.1: Knowledge Cartridge Setup 261

LIMINARY

"In the realm of safety, every journey begins with a single step towards vigilance."

His work aims to describe the knowledge cartridge for homeland and territorial security, which leverages the artificial intelligence and big data engine, Aitek. The book begins by introducing the reader to the key functionalities of the Aitek AI engine, explains what a knowledge cartridge is, and then focuses on the features and implementation of the Homeland security knowledge cartridge. This cartridge autonomously manages internal security issues through the use of artificial intelligence. Furthermore, the Homeland++ extension, equipped with IoT Boxes and drones, facilitates automatic verification and targeted search for individuals or vehicles. Additionally, the territorial knowledge cartridge addresses automatic management of territorial security and the protection of sensitive areas such as borders, mining sites, nuclear power plants, and maritime terminals.

This publication is a continuation of my previous works, notably "Innovation Unleashed," which serves as the conceptual manual for Aitek 6, and "Security and Human Factor," based on my course taught at the Institute for the Fight Against Economic Crime (ILCE). The latter forms the foundation of the cybersecurity knowledge cartridge. Through these writings, my goal is to provide both a theoretical and practical framework that highlights technological innovations in security and defense, while emphasizing the critical importance of the human factor in the effective deployment of these advanced technologies.

INTRODUCTION

"A strong start is half the battle."

In this revised and expanded version, it's critical to appreciate that we introduce two principal products: the Aitek platform and the Knowledge Cartridge. The Aitek platform is an expansive collection of functionalities and technical frame-works engineered to deploy an AI-enhanced management environment without necessitating additional development. Thanks to its own methodology, it is powered by an AI agent generated by the platform, which is fueled by the meticulous governance of big data. The Knowledge Cartridge, conversely, is a specialized configuration of the platform, precisely tailored for specific industry requirements, enabling organizations to achieve mastery over their operational processes through pro-found industry insights.

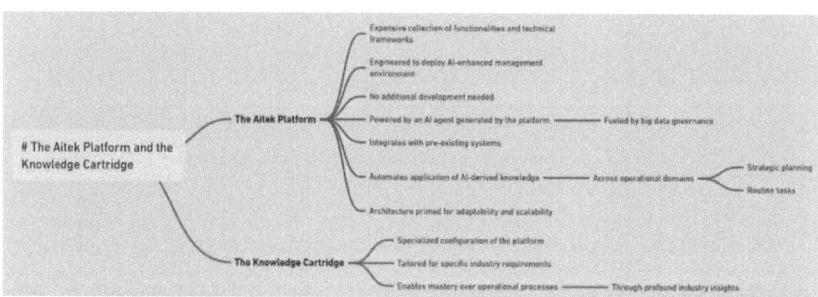

The Aitek platform represents a comprehensive solution designed to facilitate the application of artificial intelligence (AI) within various organizational frameworks, entirely circumventing the need for data scientists or software engineers. This platform is not merely an assembly of tools; it is an integrated ecosystem, complete with a proprietary methodology that seamlessly melds with an organization's pre-existing systems. It empowers the automatic application of AI-derived knowledge across a spectrum of operational domains, from strategic planning to routine tasks, with its architecture primed for adaptability and scalability. This design philosophy ensures the platform's relevance and utility in the face of evolving organizational demands and the fluid dynamics of data ecosystems.

At its core, the Aitek platform capitalizes on the potential of big data through its vector-based analytics. Amidst the deluge of data characteristic of the digital age, the platform sets itself apart not just by aggregating extensive data sets but by deploying sophisticated analytical tools and machine learning algorithms to sift through this data, yielding practical insights. These technologies are continually refined through exposure to new data, enhancing the precision and applicability of the insights provided.

The Knowledge Cartridge offers a bespoke adaptation of the Aitek platform, devised to address distinct business needs without resorting to traditional IT development. This customization extends far beyond basic adjustments, embedding industry-specific knowledge, methodologies, and benchmarks deep within the platform's functionalities. As a result, the Knowledge Cartridge does more than deliver a custom AI solution; it serves as a compendium of industry intelligence, equipping organizations with the capabilities to navigate their sectors with unparalleled proficiency and insight.

Collectively, the Aitek platform and the Knowledge Cartridge present a synergistic pairing, combining the transformative power of AI with deep, industry-specific knowledge. This combination not only streamlines and enhances operational efficiency but also fosters innovation and leadership within industries. Through this innovative approach, the Aitek solution redefines the role of AI in business, elevating it from a mere efficiency tool to a pivotal force for growth and competitive differentiation.

Chapter 0.0: reminder - the aitek platform

"AI the silent guardian, tirelessly vigilant, transforming shadows into light "

The objective of this paper is not merely to reiterate the contents of the Aitek 6 manual but to distill its essential elements to elucidate the concept of the knowledge cartridge. Aitek represents a versatile platform featuring a semantic methodology for describing an environment, termed the 'knowledge builder'. This modeling process yields a comprehensive description and data catalog, facilitating an understanding of and interaction with the environment, weighted according to risk and performance metrics.

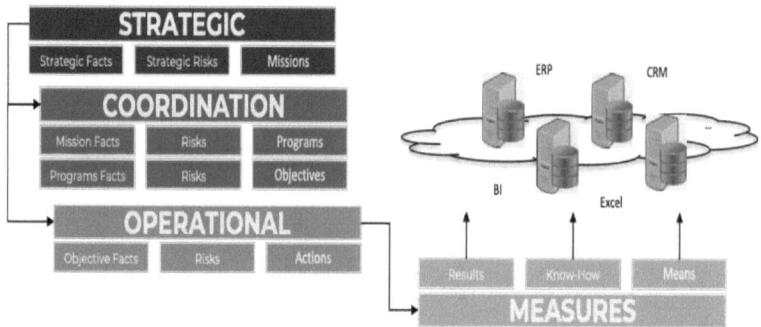

This data catalog, structured according to a performance and risk hierarchy, adopts a fractal-like logic. It spans from strategic considerations down to operational activities, categorized across three axes: outcomes, expertise, and resources, each with their temporal, analytical, and performance aggregation dimensions. The 'Data Wizard' module connects this structured framework to physical data, whether structured or unstructured, culminating in a detailed vector base description encompassing "replicat" processes, aggregation, auto-ML, clustering, and Query 360 operations.

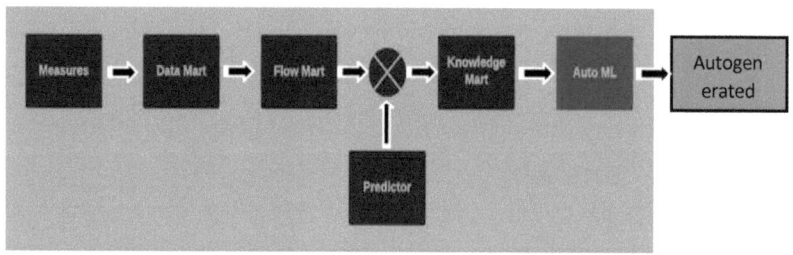

Populating the vector base unfolds in three phases:

PHASE 1:

A unified replica is created, formatting and denormalizing data to the most granular level of the model's analytical entities and cleansing the data. This phase integrates representative metadata from unstructured data into the replica.

PHASE 2:

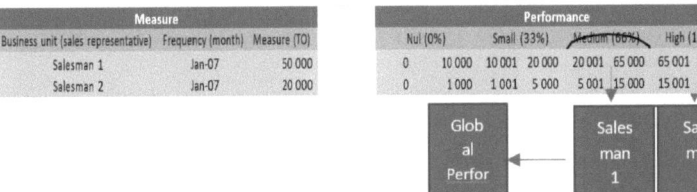

The system clusters indicators both globally and by semantic node within the model, calculating percentiles for each cluster and node, and categorizing outliers in a classified list by family within the replica. Two intelligent agents are generated for predicting each measurement/indicator and percentile. These agents extend the model with one agent per cluster and another for the entire dataset. Initially, the system evaluates and selects the optimal algorithm from our library based on the accuracy rate. Each prediction runs two algorithms in parallel, with the result being a weighted average, akin to a random forest algorithmic approach.

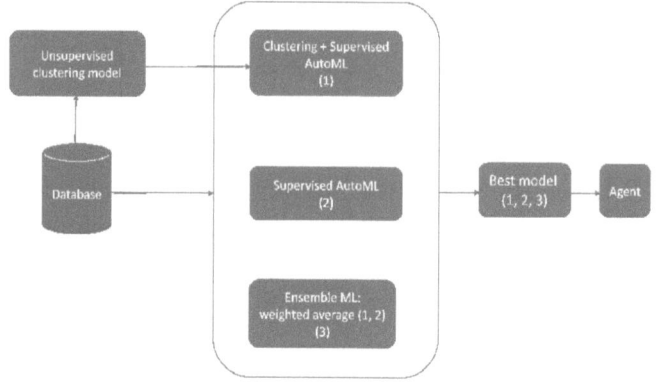

PHASE 3:

Flowmarts are created as types of datamarts through aggregation by the model's entities on a daily, monthly, quarterly, and yearly basis from the replica, loaded into a PostgreSQL-type DBMS. Outliers are also loaded into DBMS tables.

This detailed framework for the knowledge cartridge within Aitek not only showcases the platform's robustness in handling and analyzing complex datasets but also demonstrates its pioneering approach to semantic AI modeling and data management, paving the way for advanced analytical capabilities in various operational contexts.

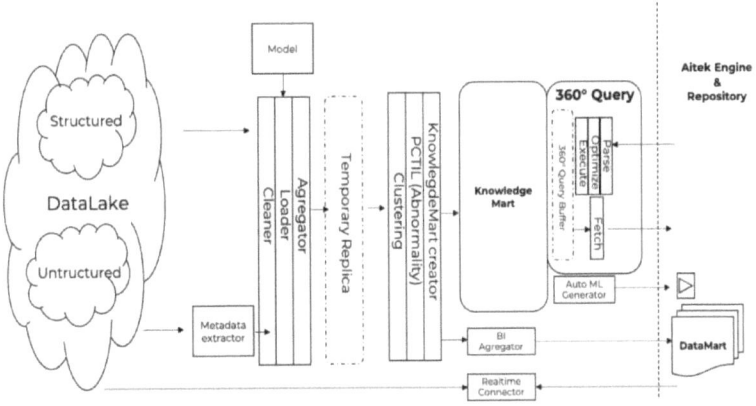

In our proposed model, a notable innovation is the mechanism to address the absence of specific indicators within the datalake. The system initiates an automated process to generate order entries and corresponding SQL tables, effectively creating a dynamic linkage to the datalake. This ensures the model's adaptability and scalability by allowing for the seamless integration of emerging data sources, thereby maintaining its relevance and utility over time.

Furthermore, the model integrates a sophisticated system for capturing both analogic and digital data emanating from a variety of sensors and cameras. These devices are interfaced with an IoT Box, which in turn is connected to a dedicated data replica. This architecture facilitates the aggregation of data across all IoT Boxes within the same category, promoting a cohesive data analysis framework.

Each IoT Box is constructed as a cluster of three nano PCs, typified by Raspberry Pi units, serving distinct functions: data acquisition and preprocessing, data processing, and data storage and communication. The architecture of the IoT Box is designed to ensure efficient data handling, from initial capture through to analysis and storage.

At the core of the data processing unit is a four-layer neural network, tailored to classify outputs into four categories: alarms, verification requirements, errors, or non-issues. This neural network architecture is pivotal for the system's ability to share or update its knowledge base. It achieves this through the transmission of a weight matrix of the neurons to the IoT Box, which then applies gradient descent for optimization.

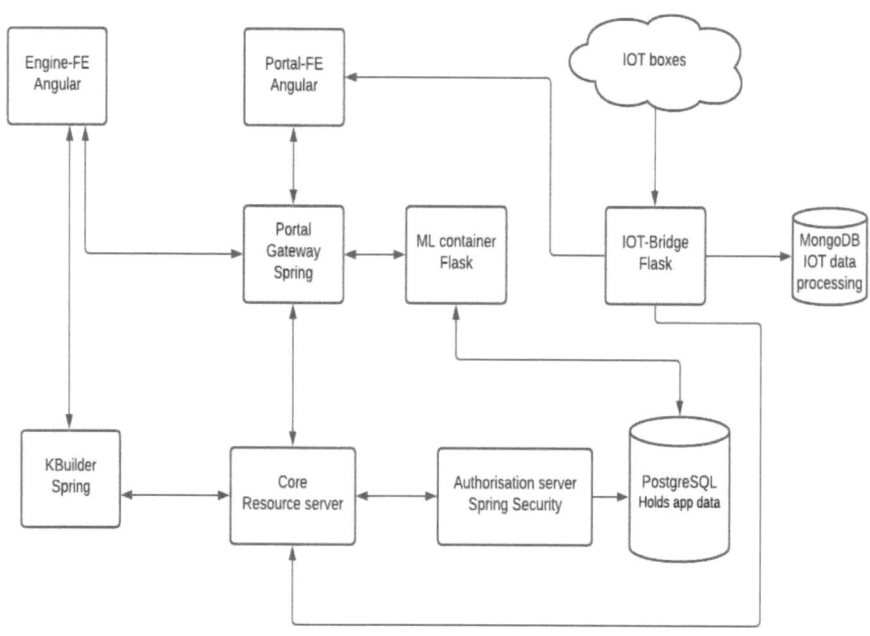

The employment of a four-layer neural network is strategic, providing a balance between complexity and computational efficiency. This design enables the rapid processing of data and the generation of actionable insights, with the added capability of knowledge transfer and updating. The IoT Box's processing unit does not independently learn; instead, it applies updates received from the central system, ensuring consistency and accuracy across the network.

This integrated system exemplifies a forward-thinking approach to data analysis, combining the Internet of Things (IoT) with advanced machine learning techniques. The result is a robust framework capable of processing vast amounts of data in real-time, while also possessing the flexibility to adapt to new data sources and analytical requirements. This innovation holds significant potential for applications requiring real-time data analysis and decision-making, offering a scalable and adaptable solution in the ever-evolving landscape of data science.

In the supervisor module, the semantic tree of the model translates percentiles into percentages of performance and risk. The proportion of outliers within the cluster associated with the business interpretation node is converted into a probability percentage. The count of indicators not linked to the information flow provides a measure of completeness. The model is constructed top-down, from mission to activity, whereas the calculation and propagation of performance/risk metrics move bottom-up, from the indicator level to the mission. Additionally, the system offers a generic dashboard creation tool with forecasting and simulation capabilities.

The system employs a pattern based on a combination of performance percentages for each model node, termed a diagnostic. The interface allows for manual generation of these diagnostics.

Anomalies are processed according to settings defined for each model node. For each type of outlier, an alarm is configured, which, depending on its type (manually or automatically dismissible), is connected to an action plan. An action plan comprises a set of actions and phases executed by designated individuals or resources within a theoretical timeframe. The transition from one phase to another occurs either automatically, after a set duration (timer), based on feedback from an AI program, upon detecting a file or specific information within a file, receiving an email, or via a voice over IP call. This structured approach ensures a comprehensive and responsive system capable of adapting to dynamic operational environments, offering a sophisticated framework for managing performance and risk across various organizational levels.

In the diagnostic component, which acts as a "geographic" distance based on combinations of performance metrics within the model, aggregates information using percentile bases. Each diagnostic is linked to two types of alarms: a preventative alarm and a corrective alarm, each connected to its respective action plan, for prevention and correction respectively.

If the "similarity" score falls between 60% and 70%, the system activates the preventative alarm. Should the score exceed this range, the corrective alarm is triggered. This mechanism ensures that potential issues are addressed proactively before escalating, while more severe discrepancies prompt immediate corrective measures to mitigate risks and optimize operational efficiency. This dual-alarm system facilitates a nuanced approach to managing operational dynamics, allowing for both anticipatory adjustments and direct interventions as dictated by the evolving situational context.

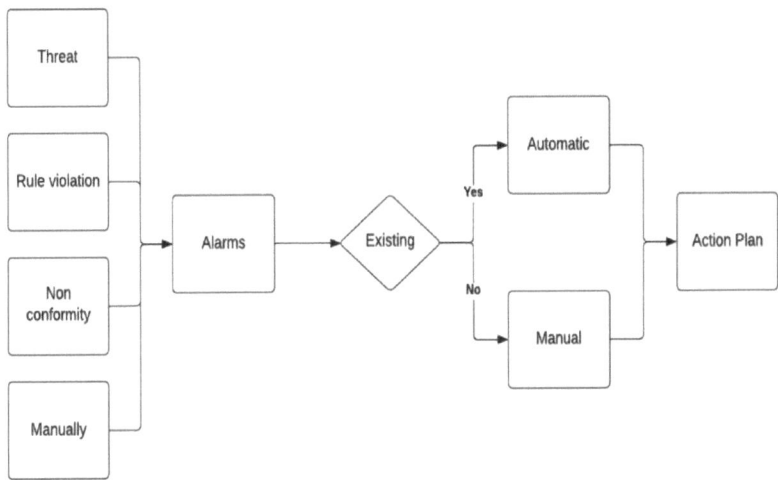

For the diagnostic component, which acts as a "geographic" distance based on combinations of performance metrics within the model, information is aggregated based on percentile rankings. Each diagnostic is linked to two alarms: a preventative alarm and a corrective alarm, with each connected to its specific action plan, for prevention and correction, respectively.

When the "similarity" falls between 60% and 70%, the system activates the preventative alarm. If the similarity exceeds this threshold, the corrective alarm is engaged. It's crucial to note that any action plan can be scheduled to trigger at a specific time (dd.mm.yyyy hh:mm:ss), but this necessitates assigning the necessary resources for that date and the theoretical duration of the action plan.

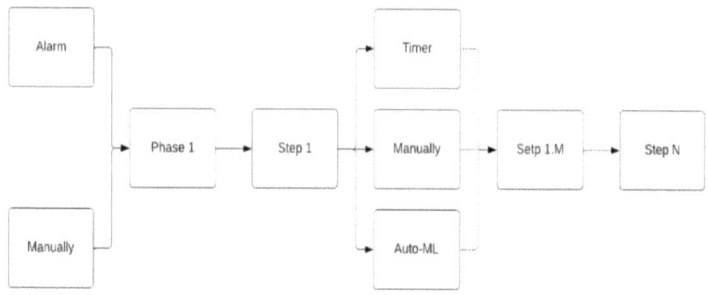

Upon the activation of an action plan, the responsible party allocates resources, and the AI suggests available resources of each required type. For certain action plans, the AI can be configured to automatically assign resources and dispatch mission orders to everyone involved, including the plan's overseer.

The AI updates a resource planning schedule (human, financial, and material) that is visible through filters in either a Gantt/PERT chart or calendar format. This system ensures efficient resource management and timely action plan execution, enabling a proactive and responsive approach to operational challenges.

The Aitek vector base is a complex structure composed of four sub-bases, designed to systematically enhance and evolve through continuous improvement following the Deming PDCA (Plan-Do-Check-Act) cycle. This scientific approach is not only innovative but also pivotal in advancing the field of artificial intelligence and big data analytics.

The first sub-base, known as the "DO" base, establishes the foundation of this system. It acts as a bridge, structuring the vast and often chaotic datalake into coherent vectors aligned with a semantic model. This structuration is critical for transforming raw data into a format that is not only manageable but also meaningful and directly linked to the operational objectives of the system.

Once the "DO" phase is implemented, the system enters a dynamic state, characterized by its alarms and action plans. Information derived from these alarms and diagnostics—because they are tethered to the semantic model—gets reintegrated into the datalake, ensuring coherence and relevance. This reintegration process corresponds to the "CHECK" sub-base, where the system evaluates its performance and the efficacy of its responses.

Subsequent to the "CHECK" phase, the "ACT" sub-base comes into play. Here, information generated by the execution of action plans linked to the model is gathered. This not only includes the outcomes of these plans but also the insights and learnings derived from their application. This iterative learning process is fundamental to the PDCA cycle, facilitating not just correction but also innovation.

Finally, the "PLAN" sub-base encapsulates the resources and time series data that supported the execution of action plans. By integrating these elements in a coherent manner, the system ensures that all operational activities are rooted in strategic planning and informed decision-making.

The amalgamation of these four sub-bases—underpinned by auto-ML algorithms and pattern recognition—enables the AI to self-improve and evolve. This self-ameliorating mechanism is designed to refine the system's performance continuously, ensuring it becomes more effective and efficient over time. By leveraging the PDCA cycle, the Aitek vector base exemplifies how structured, data-driven approaches can revolutionize the capability of AI systems to adapt and thrive in complex operational environments.

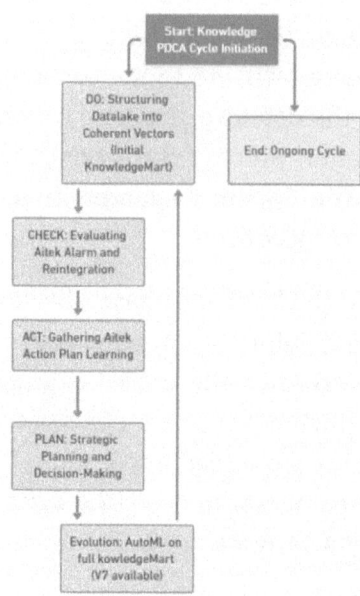

The Query 360 functionality within AITEK's solution provides users with a powerful tool to access a vast amount of data quickly and accurately, enabling comprehensive information retrieval, such as all the relevant information associated with a specific individual or entity.

When a user initiates a Query 360 request, they specify a defined time period and an analysis key that serves as a search criterion. The system then begins the search process by examining the elements present in the burn list. This list contains "sensitive" elements that are not intended to be visible to everyone but still remain in the database for analysis and machine learning purposes.

Following this initial step, a series of subsequent actions, including dispatching, execution, and fetching, are performed to obtain the desired elements and store them in a separate database. This dedicated database acts as a display interface, presenting the retrieved data to the user in a structured and organized manner.

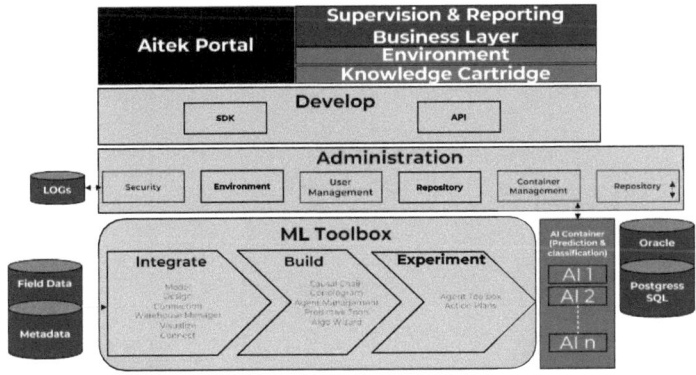

In parallel with the Query 360 execution, a report is generated that summarizes the data retrieved from the Query. This report provides a comprehensive overview of the information accessed during the Query 360 process, offering insights, trends, and analysis related to the specified time period and analysis key.

The Query 360 functionality enables users to access a wide range of data efficiently and effectively, facilitating in-depth analysis and informed decision-making. By leveraging the burn list to ensure data privacy and security, users can confidently explore and retrieve relevant information while maintaining appropriate data governance. The accompanying report adds value by providing a concise summary of the retrieved data, further enhancing the user's understanding and enabling them to derive actionable insights from the Query 360 results.

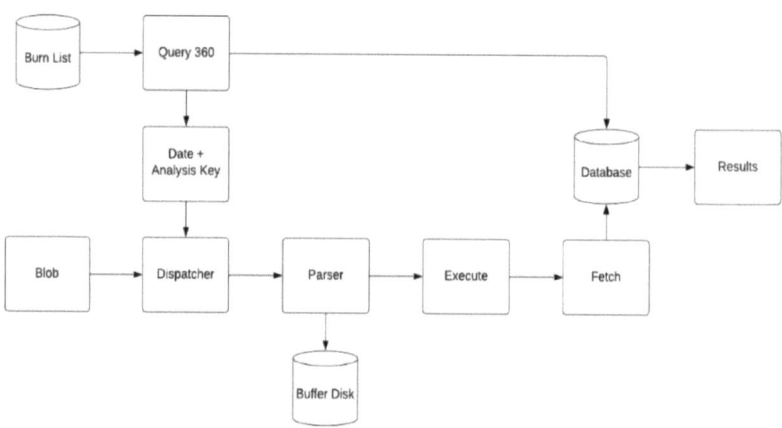

KNOWLEDGEMART SHARING

In the realm of enhancing organizational security measures, the sharing of data between entities has emerged as a critical strategy. To address this need, Aitek has innovated a system inspired by the principles of the "Schengen system," designed to streamline the process of data sharing among organizations. This chapter explores the architecture and operational mechanisms of this shared vector database system, emphasizing its role in facilitating the exchange of selected data vectors or sub-vectors among authorized organizations.

The Concept of a Shared Vector Database: at the core of Aitek's solution is the shared vector database, a centralized repository that enables the sharing and access of data vectors or sub-vectors among participating organizations. This section delves into the design principles of the shared vector database, outlining how it mirrors the Schengen system's openness within a controlled and secure framework.

Security Measures and Data Access Control: implementing stringent security protocols is paramount to ensuring that only authorized parties can access the shared data. This part of the chapter examines the security measures in place, including encryption, access controls, and authentication mechanisms, to safeguard the data from unauthorized access or misuse.

Rights and Authorizations for Data Sharing: central to the operation of the shared vector database is the system of rights and authorizations that governs data access and usage. This section details the process by which organizations are granted specific permissions to view and utilize the shared data, emphasizing the criteria and considerations involved in granting these rights.

Selective Data Sharing and Relevance: The decision-making process surrounding which data to share is critical and is undertaken with meticulous care by each participating organization. The criteria for selecting data for sharing are explored, focusing on the relevance and utility of the data in enhancing security measures across the collaborative network.

Collaboration and Enhanced Security Through Data Sharing: the shared vector database system represents a significant advancement in collaborative security efforts, enabling organizations to pool their resources, knowledge, and data to collectively enhance security measures. This section discusses the benefits of such collaboration, including improved data analysis, shared expertise, and a unified approach to addressing security challenges.

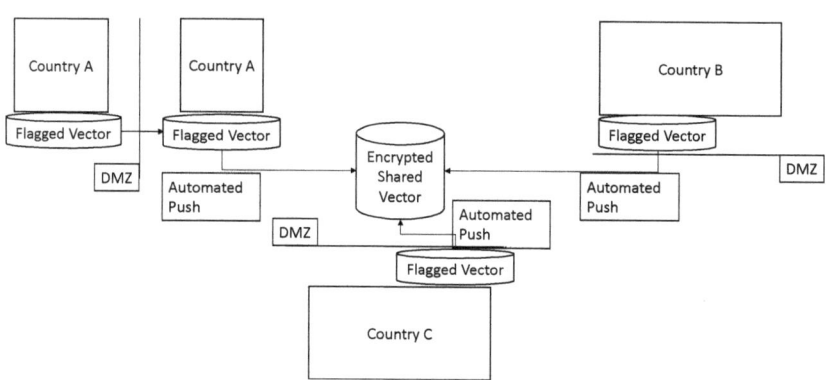

Data Security and Privacy Considerations: while the system facilitates unprecedented levels of cooperation among organizations, it also raises important considerations regarding data security and privacy. This part of the chapter addresses these concerns, detailing the safeguards and protocols in place to ensure that sensitive information is protected and that the system's integrity is maintained.

Aitek's shared vector database system, inspired by the Schengen system, marks a significant innovation in the field of organizational security. By enabling the controlled sharing of data among authorized organizations, the system enhances the collective ability to improve security measures. This chapter has provided a comprehensive overview of the system's architecture, operational mechanisms, and the careful balance it strikes between openness and security, highlighting its potential to transform collaborative security efforts while maintaining a steadfast commitment to data privacy and protection.

The Knowledge Mart within the vector database of the Aitek platform is an aggregation of data drawn from a variety of heterogeneous sources, both structured and unstructured, housed within a data lake and owned by distinct entities. For instance, in the realm of homeland security, data might originate from the central bank, air and border police, or telecommunications operators. This diversity presents a unique challenge; if an error is discovered within the returned information of a Query 360 operation, any corrective measures ("patches") applied to the Knowledge Mart during the next refresh could potentially be undone or only partially retained until the original data source addresses the error.

Aitek manages this situation through a sophisticated mechanism within its data management infrastructure. Upon identifying an error, the platform utilizes its Data Wizard module to access the source's ownership details stored within its populated dictionary. At the moment of applying an update to correct the error, a "expiration date" is assigned to the internal modification, by default set to one month. Concurrently, the system dispatches an email to the data source's owner, detailing the necessary corrections along with a deadline, also typically set for one month. This initiates a patching process for the database to correct historical data.

During the expiration period, the update process will adjust the incremental data loaded onto a temporary replica—prior to clustering and percentile calculations—to ensure the patch's impact is minimized. Beyond the expiration date, the system will remove the correction from its update mechanism, operating under the assumption that the data owner has made the requisite adjustments upstream.

This approach underscores Aitek's proactive strategy in ensuring data integrity within its KnowledgeMart. By instituting a temporary patch system coupled with an automated notification and expiration framework, Aitek navigates the complexities of managing data from diverse and autonomous sources. This methodology not only maintains the accuracy and reliability of the platform's data analytics capabilities but also encourages data source owners to promptly address and rectify identified inaccuracies. It represents a balanced collaboration between Aitek's systemic capabilities and the accountability of external data providers, thereby enhancing the overall quality and trustworthiness of the data within the platform's ecosystem.

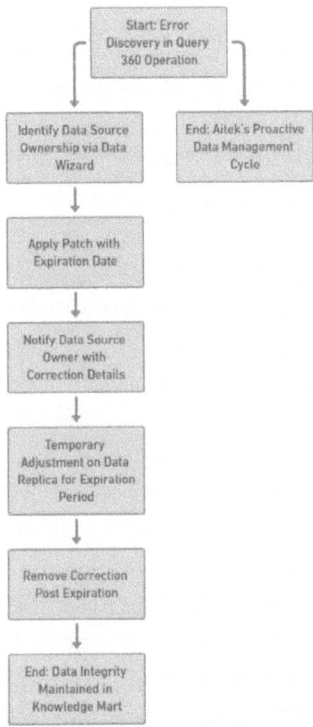

The implementation of an incremental refresh mode within a data lake environment presents a significant challenge due to the asynchronous and independent updates of data sources. Achieving coherence in the sequencing within the Knowledge Mart is crucial for maintaining data integrity and relevance. The granularity of coherence for the refresh process is determined by the timestamp of the components within the conceptual object (pre-replica). However, to ensure overall data consistency, a forced refresh of any remaining components is conducted once daily. This includes integrating the latest known versions of conceptual object components that have not been updated, thus preserving the continuity and integrity of the data.

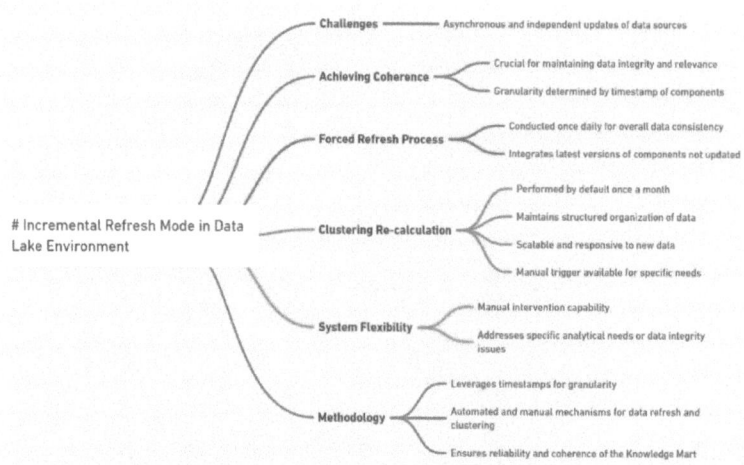

Moreover, the re-calculation of clustering on the most recent additions to the Knowledge Mart is performed by default once a month. This process is vital for maintaining the structured organization of data within the Knowledge Mart, allowing for efficient retrieval and analysis. The default monthly schedule for clustering re-calculation ensures that the system remains scalable and responsive to new data without overwhelming computational resources. However, the system offers flexibility through the ability to manually trigger this re-calculation process via an action plan. This manual intervention capability is critical for addressing specific analytical needs or data integrity issues that arise from sudden changes or additions to the data lake.

This incremental refresh strategy reflects a sophisticated approach to managing the complexities of a dynamic data environment. By leveraging timestamps for granularity and instituting both automated and manual mechanisms for data refresh and clustering re-calculation, the system ensures that the Knowledge Mart remains a reliable and coherent resource for data analysis. This methodology underscores the importance of adaptability and precision in the management of big data, enabling organizations to derive actionable insights from their data assets while maintaining high standards of data quality and integrity.

Chapter 0.1: reminder: Knowledge Cartridge

"In the domain of security: knowledge is the fortress, vigilance is its guardian."

The knowledge cartridge represents a specialized configuration set for the Aitek engine, tailored to specific industry needs and designed to be replicable. This configuration encapsulates the essence of Aitek's artificial intelligence and big data capabilities (vectoriel database), fine-tuned to address the unique challenges and opportunities within a particular sector.

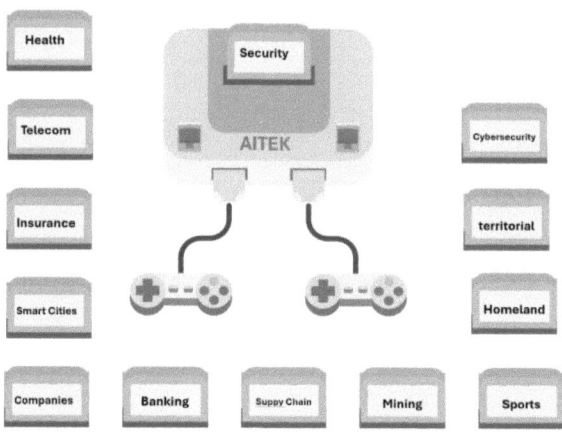

Each cartridge integrates a comprehensive suite of parameters, algorithms (generate by auto-ML), and semantic models, aligning the engine's functionality with industry-specific requirements. This enables the Aitek platform to quickly adapt to different operational contexts, ensuring that its predictive analytics, data management, and decision-support tools are directly relevant to the targeted industry's needs.

The replicability of these cartridges is a crucial aspect, allowing for the rapid deployment of Aitek's technology across various sectors with minimal customization effort. This feature not only accelerates the implementation process but also ensures consistency in performance and outcomes across different applications.

By leveraging the knowledge cartridge approach, businesses can harness the power of AI and big data analytics without the need for extensive reconfiguration or development from scratch. This method provides a scalable, efficient pathway to digital transformation, enabling organizations to stay at the forefront of innovation in their respective industries.

This involves the semantic model, encompassing generic strategic requirements, the standard organization of business units, and classic professions implicated in the industry. It also requires a deep understanding of the risks, processes, and operational and support activities specific to the concerned industry. Additionally, it's essential to know how, in best practices, the desired impact is measured (Results), that execution follows best practices (Know-how), and that resources are utilized optimally (Means).

Identifying relevant analysis entities and optimal business aggregation entities is crucial. These should be significant enough to ensure that the flowmarts and diagnostics are comprehensive. This step involves creating the knowledge builder. This part must be completed in close collaboration with one or more industry experts and an expert in the Aitek methodology. The quality of the model will directly correlate with the quality of the knowledge cartridge, underlining the importance of expert input in shaping the semantic structure and ensuring the cartridge's effectiveness in addressing industry-specific challenges.

We will connect through the Data Wizard to a generic CSV file-based data lake, covering all indicators of the model. Then, we generate the diagnostics, alarms, and action plans as generically as possible yet as representative of the domain's customs and necessary standard resources by creating the catalog through the engine's front end (the parameter setter, different from the end-users' supervisor). An initial set of dashboards is created.

Subsequently, a technical team generates data to coherently populate one year's data for a sample representing at least 25% of the production volume using either a Python program or a standard generator for all the CSV files. Engineers will then introduce anomalies, inconsistencies, outliers, etc., into the files, documenting them.

Following this, we generate the vector base with the implementation of the "DO" base from the generated CSV files. We check the coherence of alarms, dashboards, action plans, and resource planning. Finally, we document the supervisor screens in a manual for end-users, providing a comprehensive guide to navigating and utilizing the system effectively.

The comprehensive knowledge cartridge package is meticulously assembled into an encrypted archive, utilizing advanced encryption standards to safeguard its contents. The encryption employs a dual-key system, where the public key is derived from the unique version number assigned to the knowledge cartridge, ensuring specificity and version control. Conversely, the private key, essential for decrypting the contents, is uniquely generated based on the serial number provided exclusively to the client, ensuring a personalized and secure distribution.

Contained within this encrypted archive are several critical components essential for the deployment and operation of the Aitek platform within a specific industry context. These components include:

Knowledge Builder: the core framework that establishes the semantic model, detailing strategic requirements, organizational structures, and standard business units pertinent to the industry. This builder lays the foundation for the Aitek engine, enabling it to understand and interact with the environment in an industry-specific manner.

Data Wizard: a sophisticated tool designed to seamlessly integrate and structure data from a diverse range of sources into the platform. It connects the Aitek engine to an industry-specific datalake, typically comprising generic CSV files that span the entire spectrum of indicators identified in the semantic model.

Alarms and Action Plans: predefined alerts and corresponding response strategies formulated to address potential anomalies, risks, or operational inefficiencies detected by the Aitek engine. These are crafted to be as generic yet representative as possible, embodying standard practices and resources within the industry.

Dashboards: a set of user interfaces and visualization tools developed to provide end-users with real-time insights, performance metrics, and risk assessments derived from the analysis conducted by the Aitek engine. These dashboards are designed for intuitive navigation and are documented thoroughly for user reference.

Test Datasets: a collection of artificially generated data designed to populate the system with coherent information spanning a year, representing at least 25% of the production volume. This dataset includes documented anomalies, inconsistencies, and outliers to test and validate the system's diagnostic capabilities.

Technical Documentation: comprehensive manuals and guides that detail the operation of the supervisor interface for end-users, explaining how to interpret alarms, manage action plans, and utilize dashboards effectively.

Encryption Keys: the package includes detailed instructions on how to decrypt the archive, facilitating access to the knowledge cartridge while maintaining the highest security standards.

Each element of the package is encrypted and compiled with precision, ensuring that upon receipt, the client possesses all necessary tools, documentation, and resources to implement, train, and operate the Aitek platform effectively within their specific industrial domain. This approach not only secures the intellectual property contained within the cartridge but also facilitates a streamlined deployment process tailored to the client's specific needs and operational context.

For the installation of the cartridge and the loading of the supervisor, it is necessary to enter the license key and the address of the data lake's virtual machine (VM). This process facilitates the cartridge setup along with a sandbox environment for initial testing and exploration. Following the installation, the next step involves navigating to the Data

Wizard tool to establish a production vector database. This requires configuring the data lake's VM address and adjusting settings to accommodate data sourced from various formats such as CSV files, databases, or other data storage solutions. To initiate the creation of the vector database, the system prompts a forced re-learning process to adapt the Aitek engine to the specific data environment and operational parameters set forth by the user. This procedure ensures that the system is finely tuned to the industry-specific requirements encapsulated within the knowledge cartridge, enabling a seamless transition from a generic setup to a fully customized and operational AI and big data platform.

PART 1:
Homeland Security with Aitek

"In the homeland security, AI is the guardian at the gate"

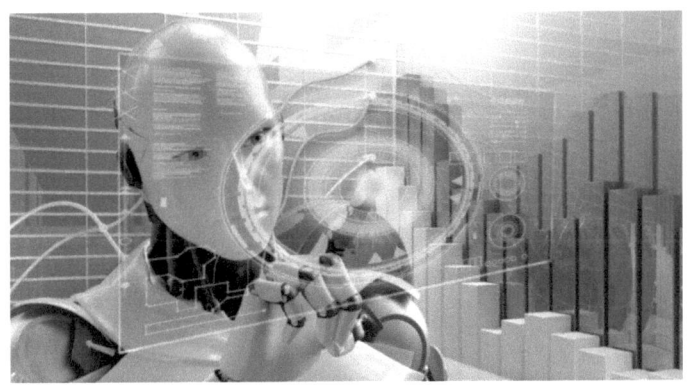

Chapter 1.0: homeland security concept

"An ounce of prevention is worth a pound of cure"

The primary missions of homeland security encompass combating terrorism, suppressing any form of foreign interference, safeguarding the nation's economic and scientific heritage, countering cyber threats, and preventing the proliferation of weapons of mass destruction. These core objectives are pivotal in ensuring the safety and integrity of a nation, employing a comprehensive and multifaceted approach to address a wide range of security challenges that modern societies face. Through strategic planning, collaboration across various sectors, and the integration of advanced technologies, homeland security efforts aim to protect citizens, infrastructure, and critical national interests from both internal and external threats.

Combating terrorism within the realm of homeland security using Artificial Intelligence (AI) involves the deployment of advanced algorithms and machine learning techniques to predict, detect, and neutralize terrorist threats. AI enhances homeland security's capabilities in several key areas:

Predictive Analysis: AI can analyze vast amounts of data from various sources, including social media, intelligence reports, and surveillance footage, to identify patterns and predict potential terrorist activities before they occur. By leveraging predictive modeling, security agencies can forecast terrorist attacks with greater accuracy and take preemptive measures.

Surveillance and Monitoring: AI-powered systems enable continuous monitoring of digital communications, financial transactions, and movements of suspected individuals or groups. Facial recognition technologies and drones equipped with AI can identify suspects in crowded places, track their movements, and alert authorities to suspicious activities.

Data Integration and Analysis: AI systems can integrate and analyze data from diverse sources, including immigration records, flight manifests, and biometric databases, to identify potential threats. This holistic view enables security agencies to make informed decisions based on comprehensive risk assessments.

Counter-radicalization: AI can also aid in identifying and addressing the online spread of extremist ideologies. By monitoring social media and other online platforms, AI systems can detect radical content, track its spread, and help in the development of counter-narratives to prevent radicalization.

Autonomous Security Systems: AI-driven robots and drones can perform surveillance and reconnaissance missions in dangerous or inaccessible areas, reducing the risk to human personnel and increasing the efficiency of security operations.

Decision Support: AI can assist decision-makers by providing them with real-time insights, threat assessments, and recommendations, enabling them to make faster, more informed decisions in crisis situations.

Incorporating AI into homeland security strategies significantly enhances the ability to combat terrorism by improving threat detection, response times, and the overall effectiveness of security measures. However, it also raises ethical and privacy concerns that need to be carefully managed.

Foreign interference in homeland security, especially in the context of AI (Artificial Intelligence), can take various forms, reflecting the complex and evolving landscape of global threats. AI, with its vast capabilities, becomes both a tool and a target in these scenarios. Here are some ways foreign interference might manifest:

Cyber Espionage: Using AI algorithms, foreign entities can conduct sophisticated cyber espionage operations to steal sensitive information, intellectual property, and state secrets. AI can enhance the capabilities of malware, making it smarter and harder to detect.

Disinformation Campaigns: AI can generate deepfakes or synthetic media that are increasingly realistic and difficult to differentiate from authentic content. Such technologies can be used to manipulate public opinion, interfere in elections, or sow discord within a society.

AI-Powered Hacking: Automated systems powered by AI can carry out hacking attempts at a scale and speed far beyond human capabilities. These can include brute force attacks, vulnerability discovery, and the exploitation of networks and systems.

Surveillance and Reconnaissance: foreign entities might use AI for advanced surveillance and reconnaissance, employing facial recognition technologies and other forms of biometric surveillance to track individuals, understand security protocols, or gather intelligence on critical infrastructure.

Autonomous Attack Drones and Robotics: in military contexts, foreign interference might involve the use of AI-powered autonomous drones or robotic systems designed to carry out attacks or reconnaissance without direct human control, posing new challenges for homeland security.

Influence and Control of AI Infrastructure: gaining control over or influencing the AI infrastructure and systems of another nation can provide a significant strategic advantage. This might include sabotage of AI systems, insertion of backdoors in AI software, or manipulation of AI training data to compromise the system's integrity.

Social Engineering and Psychological Operations: AI can analyze vast amounts of data to identify vulnerabilities in a population's psyche, enabling targeted social engineering attacks and psychological operations designed to destabilize a society or manipulate its citizens.

In response to these threats, homeland security efforts increasingly incorporate AI into their defense mechanisms, using AI for threat detection, analysis, and prediction to counteract the sophisticated strategies employed by foreign entities. The race to harness AI for both offense and defense in the realm of cybersecurity and homeland security is ongoing, highlighting the need for robust ethical guidelines, international cooperation, and continued vigilance.

Safeguarding a nation's economic and scientific heritage through homeland security with Artificial Intelligence (AI) involves deploying advanced AI technologies to protect and preserve the economic assets and scientific advancements that are crucial to a nation's prosperity and global standing. This multidimensional approach focuses on several key areas:

Counterintelligence: AI can assist in identifying and countering espionage activities aimed at stealing valuable economic and scientific information. Through the analysis of vast amounts of data and communications, AI systems can uncover suspicious patterns and links between entities that may indicate espionage activities, helping to prevent the theft of intellectual property and trade secrets.

Supply Chain Security: AI technologies can monitor and secure supply chains, ensuring the safe and uninterrupted flow of goods and materials crucial to the economy and scientific research. AI-driven logistics and anomaly detection systems can identify risks and vulnerabilities in the supply chain, from manufacturing to distribution, and suggest mitigation strategies to prevent disruptions.

Fraud Detection: in the economic sector, AI systems are employed to detect and prevent fraudulent activities that can have severe financial implications. By analyzing transaction patterns and financial data, AI can identify irregularities that may signify fraud, insider trading, or other financial crimes, thereby protecting the economic health of the nation.

Research and Development (R&D) Enhancement: AI can acce-lerate scientific research and development, fostering inno-vation and ensuring a nation's competitiveness in the global arena. AI-driven data analysis, simulation, and modeling tools can enhance research efficiency, uncover new insights, and streamline the R&D process, contributing to the advancement of national scientific endeavors.

Disaster Response and Economic Recovery: AI can play a crucial role in responding to natural disasters and economic crises by analyzing data to predict outcomes, optimize resource allocation, and plan recovery efforts. AI-driven models can help predict economic impacts and guide policymakers in crafting strategies for economic resilience and recovery.

In conclusion, safeguarding a nation's economic and scientific heritage through homeland security with AI is about leve-raging the power of advanced technologies to protect against threats, foster innovation, and ensure the economic and scientific pillars of a nation remain strong and resilient against all forms of disruption.

Countering cyber threats in homeland security with Artificial Intelligence (AI) involves leveraging advanced AI technologies to detect, prevent, and respond to cyber attacks that could endanger national security. This approach is critical because cyber threats are becoming increasingly sophisticated, with attackers using complex methods to bypass traditional se-curity measures. Here's how AI contributes to countering these threats:

Threat Detection and Prediction: AI algorithms can analyze vast amounts of data from various sources in real-time to identify patterns and anomalies indicative of cyber threats. Machine learning models can learn from historical cyber attack data, enabling them to predict potential future attacks before they occur.

Automated Response: once a threat is detected, AI systems can automatically initiate responses to mitigate the attack without human intervention. This rapid response is crucial for minimizing damage, especially in attacks that spread quickly, such as ransomware.

Network Behavior Analysis: AI can monitor network behavior continuously, learning what normal behavior looks like and flagging any deviations. This capability is essential for detecting insider threats and advanced persistent threats (APTs) that traditional security tools might overlook.

Enhancing Cybersecurity Measures: AI can improve existing cybersecurity measures by optimizing firewall rules, updating antivirus definitions in real-time, and adjusting security policies to better protect against identified threats.

Phishing Detection: AI models are trained to recognize the characteristics of phishing emails and websites, which are often used as entry points for more significant attacks. By identifying and blocking these attempts, AI helps prevent breaches that could lead to more severe security incidents.

Vulnerability Management: AI can help in identifying vulnerabilities within a system or network by continuously scanning and analyzing the infrastructure for known and emerging vulnerabilities. This proactive approach allows for timely patching and remediation efforts.

Security Information and Event Management (SIEM): integrating AI into SIEM systems enhances their ability to analyze security logs and alerts from various sources, making it easier to identify genuine threats among the vast amount of security data generated in large networks.

By incorporating AI into homeland security strategies, countries can significantly enhance their ability to detect and respond to cyber threats, making their digital infrastructure more resilient against attacks. This technological advancement allows for more sophisticated and adaptive cybersecurity measures that can keep pace with the evolving threat landscape.

In the realm of cybersecurity, there exists a specialized knowledge cartridge, detailed in a dedicated publication. The Homeland Security cartridge we've developed focuses exclusively on counter-terrorism and criminal organization aspects. As of its 2024 version, it does not address foreign interference, the protection of the nation's economic and scientific heritage, cyber threat mitigation, or the proliferation of weapons of mass destruction. This delineation underscores the cartridge's tailored approach to specific security challenges, leaving the broader spectrum of national security concerns to be addressed by other specialized cartridges or systems designed for those purposes.

The development of the knowledge cartridge represents a sophisticated approach to enhancing security protocols through advanced data analysis and behavioral assessment. This system operates by aggregating a wide range of information from various sources, utilizing both structured and unstructured data to construct a comprehensive profile of behaviors that signify potential threats. The process involves several key stages:

Data Collection: the initial phase involves an extensive collection of data, encompassing digital footprints, communication patterns, financial transactions, and other relevant activities. This data is sourced from a myriad of platforms, including social media, public records, and surveillance systems, ensuring a multidimensional view of individuals and groups.

Behavioral Analysis: utilizing advanced algorithms and machine learning techniques, the system analyzes the collected data to identify behavioral patterns and trends. This analysis focuses on detecting anomalies or signs of hostility that deviate from standard behavioral norms. The AI-driven component of the cartridge is capable of discerning subtle indications of hostile intent, such as unusual communication patterns, financial transactions, or movement behaviors that align with known profiles of threat actors.

Risk Assessment: upon identifying potential hostile behaviors, the system categorizes individuals or groups based on the level of threat they pose. This risk assessment is critical for prioritizing responses and allocating resources effectively. It employs a dynamic scoring system that evaluates the immediacy and severity of the threat, factoring in both current behavior and historical data to forecast potential actions.

Homeland Security Missions and AI Integration

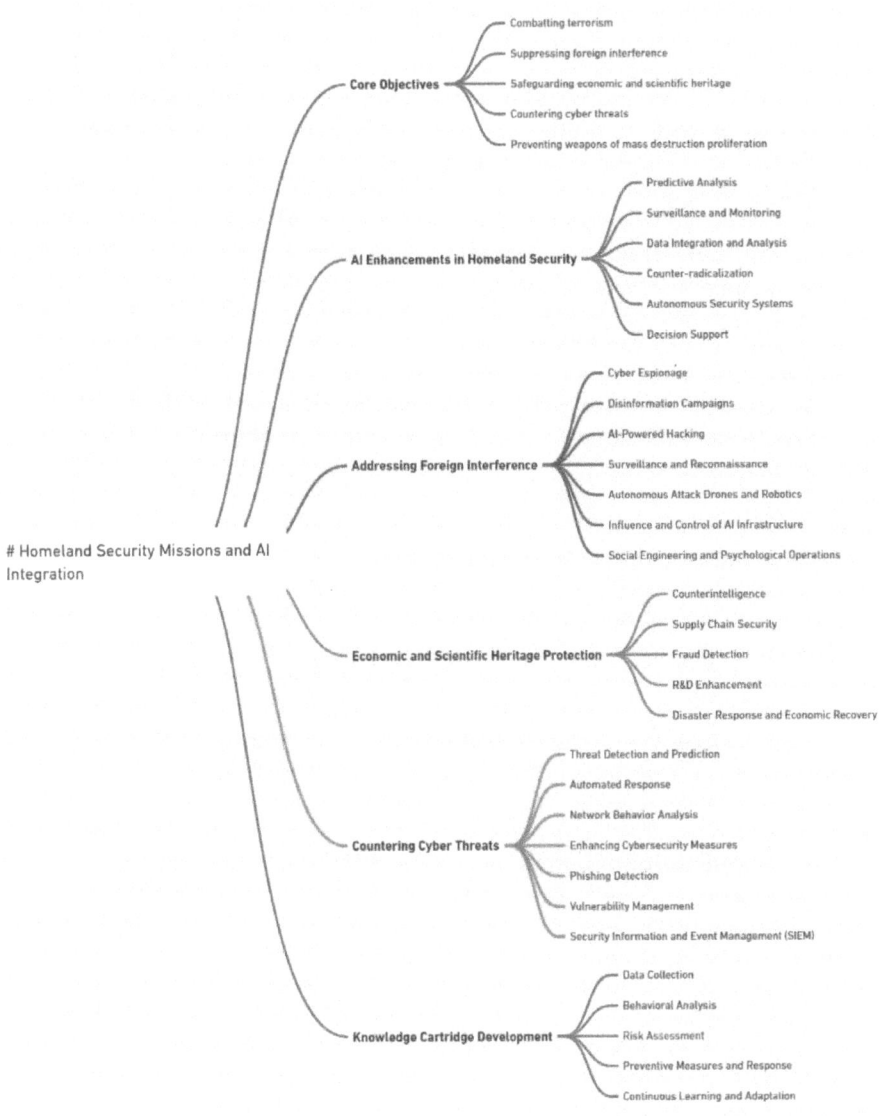

Preventive Measures and Response: with the identification and prioritization of threats, the cartridge facilitates the implementation of preventive measures. This could include increased surveillance, direct intervention by security forces, or community outreach programs aimed at deterring individuals from adopting hostile paths. In cases where an imminent attack is anticipated, the system enables a rapid response strategy, mobilizing resources to neutralize the threat before it materializes.

Continuous Learning and Adaptation: the knowledge cartridge is designed for continuous improvement, learning from each incident and interaction to enhance its predictive capabilities. By analyzing outcomes and integrating feedback, the system refines its algorithms, ensuring that it remains effective against evolving security challenges.

In summary, the knowledge cartridge is a pivotal tool in the arsenal of homeland security efforts, offering a proactive and intelligent solution to identifying, assessing, and mitigating threats. Its ability to analyze complex behavioral data and anticipate hostile actions represents a significant advancement in maintaining public safety and national security.

Chapter 1.1: Homeland in Aitek: Approach

"A stitch in time saves nine."

The development of the knowledge cartridge represents a sophisticated approach to enhancing security protocols through advanced data analysis and behavioral assessment. This system operates by aggregating a wide range of information from various sources, utilizing both structured and unstructured data to construct a comprehensive profile of behaviors that signify potential threats. The process involves several key stages:

Data Collection: in the endeavor to enhance homeland security through the use of artificial intelligence (AI), the Aitek platform adopts a comprehensive approach to gather and analyze data from diverse sources. The initial phase of data collection is critical, aiming to create a detailed map of available information that reflects the complex web of interactions and activities of individuals and groups. This includes analyzing digital footprints left on various online platforms, scrutinizing communication patterns for anomalies or threats, tracking financial transactions for signs of illicit funding, and more. By aggregating data from social networks, public records, and surveillance operations, the platform can construct a multi-faceted view of potential security risks within a nation's borders.

Once this vast pool of data is collected, the next step involves filtering and processing it through the unique semantic analysis capabilities of the Aitek platform. This is where the platform's strength in handling big data comes to the forefront. Utilizing advanced algorithms and machine learning techniques, Aitek can sift through the collected information to identify patterns, trends, and anomalies that might indicate a threat to homeland security. This process is not focused on individual data points in isolation but rather on how these points connect and interact to form a coherent picture of potential security challenges.

The methodology employed by Aitek is designed to prioritize efficiency and accuracy in threat detection. By focusing on a specific program dedicated to monitoring population movements and assessing internal risks, the platform ensures that the most relevant data is analyzed in real-time. This allows for the timely identification of threats, ranging from potential terrorist activities to emerging patterns of radicalization within the population. The goal is not just to react to threats as they arise but to anticipate and prevent them through proactive surveillance and analysis.

This sophisticated approach to homeland security highlights the potential of AI and big data in safeguarding nations against a wide array of internal threats. By developing a comprehensive understanding of the data landscape and applying the Aitek methodology, security agencies can significantly enhance their ability to monitor, analyze, and respond to potential risks, thereby ensuring the safety and security of their citizens.Behavioral Analysis: Utilizing advanced algorithms and machine learning techniques, the system analyzes the collected data to identify behavioral patterns and trends. This analysis focuses on detecting anomalies or signs of hostility that deviate from standard behavioral norms. The AI-driven component of the cartridge is capable of discerning subtle indications of hostile intent, such as unusual communication patterns, financial transactions, or movement behaviors that align with known profiles of threat actors.

Risk Assessment: upon identifying potential hostile behaviors, the system categorizes individuals or groups based on the level of threat they pose. This risk assessment is critical for prioritizing responses and allocating resources effectively. It employs a dynamic scoring system that evaluates the immediacy and severity of the threat, factoring in both current behavior and historical data to forecast potential actions.

Preventive Measures and Response: with the identification and prioritization of threats, the cartridge facilitates the implementation of preventive measures. This could include increased surveillance, direct intervention by security forces, or community outreach programs aimed at deterring individuals from adopting hostile paths. In cases where an imminent attack is anticipated, the system enables a rapid response strategy, mobilizing resources to neutralize the threat before it materializes.

Continuous Learning and Adaptation: the knowledge cartridge is designed for continuous improvement, learning from each incident and interaction to enhance its predictive capabilities. By analyzing outcomes and integrating feedback, the system refines its algorithms, ensuring that it remains effective against evolving security challenges.

In summary, the knowledge cartridge is a pivotal tool in the arsenal of homeland security efforts, offering a proactive and intelligent solution to identifying, assessing, and mitigating threats. Its ability to analyze complex behavioral data and anticipate hostile actions represents a significant advancement in maintaining public safety and national security.

Focusing on these 14 axes provides a comprehensive understanding of an individual's or group's behavior within a societal context. This multidimensional approach enables the identification of patterns and anomalies that might indicate potential security threats. Here's how each axis contributes to the overall analysis:

Citizen Information: collects basic demographic and identity data, facilitating cross-reference with other datasets for a holistic view of an individual's societal interactions.

Banking Transactions: monitors financial activities to detect unusual transactions that could indicate funding for illicit activities or the financial profiling of potential threats.

Telephone Metadata: analyzes call patterns, frequencies, and connections to identify networks and communication behaviors typical of covert operations or coordination efforts.

Water and Electricity Consumption: observes utility usage to identify irregularities, such as significantly reduced consumption that might suggest a property is being used for purposes other than residency.

Taxes: examines tax records for discrepancies or anomalies that could indicate undeclared income sources or financial misconduct linked to illicit activities.

Vehicles: tracks vehicle registrations and movements, providing insights into an individual's mobility and potential for logistical support in hostile actions.

Criminal Records: reviews an individual's legal history for any indications of past behavior that might correlate with future security risks.

Political, Religious, and Association Affiliations: Assesses affiliations to understand an individual's ideological leanings and potential for involvement in extremism.

Air and Border Police Records: Monitors cross-border movements and flights to track the international mobility of individuals of interest and identify patterns related to trafficking or the movement of potential threats.

Customs Data: Analyzes import and export records associated with individuals to detect the movement of contraband or materials that could be used in acts of terror or criminal activities.

By integrating these axes into a unified analysis framework, the knowledge cartridge enables a deep dive into the data landscape of individuals and groups. This approach facilitates the early detection of potential threats by highlighting deviations from normative patterns across various facets of life and societal engagement. The synthesis of this data supports a proactive stance in homeland security efforts, allowing for timely interventions and the mitigation of risks before they can escalate into public safety incidents.

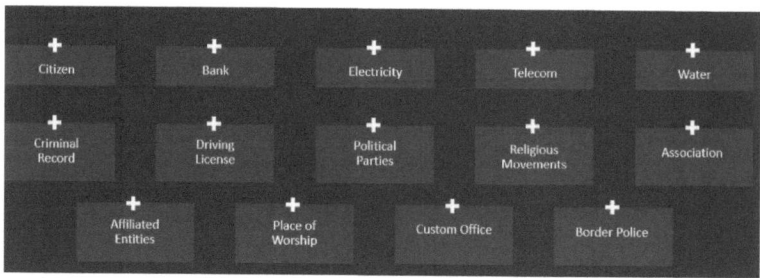

Chapter 1.2: Homeland in Aitek: Model

"Forewarned is forearmed."

The development of the knowledge cartridge represents a sophisticated approach to enhancing security protocols through Aitek basic Homeland Model

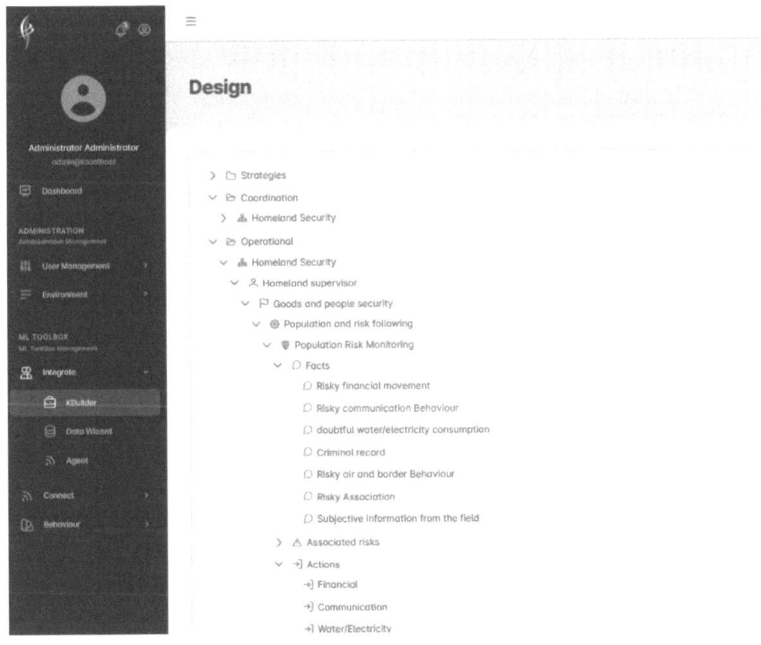

In the domain of population surveillance for the identification and isolation of hostile clusters, an advanced approach is necessitated by the complexities inherent to modern data environments. This paper outlines the implementation of a vectorial database (structured Big Data) designed to de-normalize and interlink vast arrays of information in a manner analogous to a vast Excel spreadsheet. This database architecture is specifically engineered to accommodate detailed records of banking transactions, categorized by type, date, origin (recipient), and destination (sender), as well as telecommunications behaviors including the origin and destination of calls, duration, and, notably, encrypted messaging services such as WhatsApp, Signal, and Telegram through the integration of an IoT Box dedicated to social media analysis (further details are provided later in the document).

The surveillance framework extends beyond financial and communication data to include judicial records, as well as detailed observations related to religious, political, and civic life, incorporating empirical data gathered from field operations. This comprehensive data aggregation strategy is pivotal for constructing a holistic view of societal dynamics, enabling the identification of patterns and correlations that may signify hostile intent or behavior within the population.

Banking Transactions Analysis: the analysis of banking transactions by type, date, origin, and destination offers invaluable insights into the financial flows that may underpin hostile activities. By tracing the financial transactions of individuals and entities, it is possible to uncover networks of support and funding that sustain hostile clusters, providing a basis for targeted interventions.

Telecommunications Behavior: the monitoring of telecommunications behavior, including call and message data, serves as a critical indicator of social networks and interactions. The identification of communication patterns, especially those conducted over encrypted messaging services, requires the deployment of specialized IoT Boxes capable of penetrating these secure channels to gather intelligence.

Encrypted Messaging Services: The challenge of monitoring encrypted messaging services such as WhatsApp, Signal, and Telegram is addressed through the deployment of the IoT Box for social media. This technology is designed to bypass encryption barriers to access and analyze communication data, offering a critical window into the private exchanges that could facilitate hostile activities.

Design

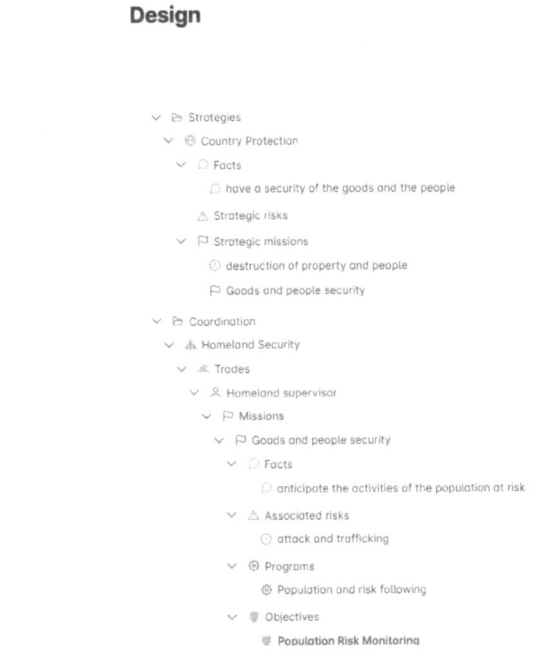

Judicial, Religious, Political, and Civic Life: The inclusion of data related to an individual's judicial history, religious affiliations, political activities, and civic engagement provides a multidimensional profile that enhances the predictive accuracy of the surveillance system. This holistic approach to data collection ensures that potential threats are identified not solely based on isolated indicators but through a comprehensive analysis of an individual's life and associations.

Empirical Field Data: the integration of empirical field data into the surveillance framework enriches the database with ground-truth observations, offering context and validation to the patterns and correlations identified through data analysis. This synergy between data-driven insights and empirical evidence is fundamental to the operational efficacy of the surveillance system.

Design

- Operational
  - Homeland Security
    - Homeland supervisor
      - Goods and people security
        - Population and risk following
          - Population Risk Monitoring
            - Facts
              - Risky financial movement
              - Risky communication Behaviour
              - doubtful water/electricity consumption
              - Criminal record
              - Risky air and border Behaviour
              - Risky Association
              - Subjective information from the field
            - Associated risks
              - Money laundering and hidden financing
              - destructive action planification
              - Illegal harboring of dangerous persons
              - dangerous action potential
              - Abroad Support
              - Criminal Association
              - Losing information about attack potential

In conclusion, the development and deployment of a vectorial database for the surveillance of populations to isolate hostile clusters represent a significant advancement in the field of security and intelligence. By de-normalizing and interlinking diverse data sources into a coherent framework, it is possible to achieve a nuanced understanding of the societal dynamics that underpin hostility, facilitating targeted interventions that are both effective and informed by a comprehensive data analysis.

Design

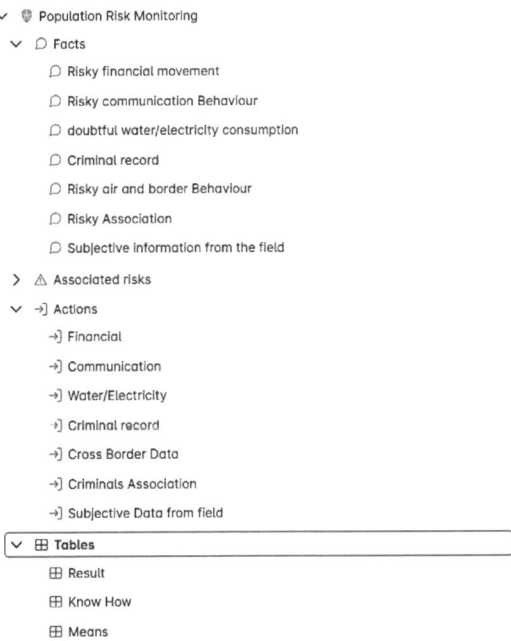

In the development of our foundational analytics cartridge, our focus has been primarily on "classic" indicators known for their accessibility and reliability across various datasets. The design of the base model was informed by two pilot studies, one conducted in Central Europe and the other in Africa. These pilots were instrumental in demonstrating the versatility and applicability of the model across diverse geographical and socio-economic contexts.

Impact / Result per activity

Cross Border Data							Weight / 142.85
							Add Qi
Text	Bg	Qt	Sc	V.	Direction	Weight	
Number of foreign criminal under custody	☐	☐	☐	☐	BIGGER_BETTER	142.85	

Criminal record							Weight / 142.85
							Add Qi
Text	Bg	Qt	Sc	V.	Direction	Weight	
number of individual recidivism	☐	☐	☐	☐	SMALLER_BETTER	142.85	

Communication							Weight / 142.85
							Add Qi
Text	Bg	Qt	Sc	V.	Direction	Weight	
Number of criminal activity	☐	☐	☐	☐	BIGGER_BETTER	142.85	

Number of criminal activity	☐	☐	☐	☐	BIGGER_BETTER	142.85	
Water/Electricity							WEIGHT - 142.85 ⊕ Add Qt
Text	Bg	Qt	Sc	V.	Direction	Weight	
number of criminal activities stopped	☐	☐	☐	☐	BIGGER_BETTER	142.85	
Subjective Data from field							WEIGHT - 142.85 ⊕ Add Qt
Text	Bg	Qt	Sc	V.	Direction	Weight	
number crime arrest by field agent	☐	☐	☐	☐	BIGGER_BETTER	142.85	
Criminals Association							WEIGHT - 142.85 ⊕ Add Qt
Text	Bg	Qt	Sc	V.	Direction	Weight	
number of group recidivism	☐	☐	☐			142.85	
Financial							WEIGHT - 142.85 ⊕ Add Qt
Text	Bg	Qt	Sc	V.	Direction	Weight	
Number of financial criminal under custody	☐	☐	☐	☐	BIGGER_BETTER	71.42	
number of financial crimes prevented	☐	☐	☐	☐	BIGGER_BETTER	71.42	

The selection of classic indicators was guided by several key considerations. First, the universality of these indicators allows for a broad applicability across different domains and industries, providing a solid foundation for initial analyses. Second, their established nature means there is a wealth of historical data available, facilitating robust model training and validation processes. Third, these indicators are generally well-understood by both technical and non-technical stakeholders, easing the interpretation and communication of analytical outcomes.

The base model's architecture is designed to be flexible, allowing for subsequent customization and refinement based on specific client needs and the unique characteristics of their operational environment. This adaptability is crucial for ensuring the model's relevance and effectiveness in addressing the particular challenges and opportunities faced by each client.

Following the initial installation of the analytics cartridge, a detailed gap analysis is conducted to identify any discrepancies between the model's assumptions and the client's reality (detailed further in subsequent sections). This gap analysis serves several critical functions. Firstly, it highlights areas where the base model may require adjustment to better align with the client's data landscape and business objectives. Secondly, it provides an opportunity to identify additional, perhaps more nuanced, indicators that could enhance the model's predictive power and insight generation capabilities. Finally, it facilitates a collaborative process between our team and the client, ensuring that the final model iteration is both highly tailored and optimally configured to deliver actionable insights.

Know-how per activity

Cross Border Data							WEIGHT : 142.85
							Add Qt
Text	Bg	Qt	Sc	V.	Direction	Weight	
Total time spent outside country	☐	☐	☐	☐	AROUND_VALUE		✎ 🗑
Number of trip	☐	☐	☐	☐			✎ 🗑
average duration spent outside country	☐	☐	☐	☐	AROUND_VALUE		✎ 🗑
speed of cross boarder behavior change	☐	☐	☐	☐			✎ 🗑

Criminal record							WEIGHT : 142.85
							Add Qt
Text	Bg	Qt	Sc	V.	Direction	Weight	
speed of criminal record behavior change	☐	☐	☐	☐			✎ 🗑

Communication

WEIGHT : 140.00

● Add Qt

Text	Bg	Qt	Sc	V.	Direction	Weight
Total call invoice	☐	☐	☐	☐	AROUND_VALUE	
Number of call	☐	☐	☐	☐	AROUND_VALUE	
speed of communication behavior change	☐	☐	☐	☐	SMALLER_BETTER	
communication likelihood	☐	☐	☐	☐	BIGGER_BETTER	
Call duration	☐	☐	☐	☐	AROUND_VALUE	
Risk call index	☐	☐	☐	☐	SMALLER_BETTER	

Water/Electricity

WEIGHT : 140.00

● Add Qt

Text	Bg	Qt	Sc	V.	Direction	Weight
Water consumption likelihood	☐	☐	☐	☐	BIGGER_BETTER	
Electricity consumption likelihood	☐	☐	☐	☐	BIGGER_BETTER	
speed of water consumption behavior change	☐	☐	☐	☐	SMALLER_BETTER	
speed of electricity behavior change	☐	☐	☐	☐	SMALLER_BETTER	

Subjective Data from Field

WEIGHT : 140.00

● Add Qt

Text	Bg	Qt	Sc	V.	Direction	Weight
insecurity feeling	☐	☐	☐	☐	SMALLER_BETTER	
speed of security feeling change	☐	☐	☐			

Criminals Association

WEIGHT : 140.00

● Add Qt

Text	Bg	Qt	Sc	V.	Direction	Weight
speed of association behavior change	☐	☐	☐	☐		

Financial

WEIGHT : 140.00

● Add Qt

Text	Bg	Qt	Sc	V.	Direction	Weight
Amount Transaction	☐	☐	☐	☐	AROUND_VALUE	
rate salary cash In	☐	☐	☐	☐	AROUND_VALUE	
speed of financial behavior change	☐	☐	☐	☐	SMALLER_BETTER	
rate salary cash out	☐	☐	☐	☐	AROUND_VALUE	
rate salary transaction	☐	☐	☐	☐	AROUND_VALUE	
Amount cash out	☐	☐	☐	☐	AROUND_VALUE	
Financial likelihood	☐	☐	☐	☐	BIGGER_BETTER	
Risk Finance index	☐	☐	☐	☐	SMALLER_BETTER	

| Amount cash in | ☐ | ☐ | ☐ | ☐ | AROUND_VALUE | | |
| Salary | ☐ | ☐ | ☐ | ☐ | AROUND_VALUE | | |

Means per Activity

Cross Border Data — WEIGHT / 142.85 — Add Qt

Text	Bg	Qt	Sc	V.	Direction	Weight		
Budget of border police	☐	☐	☐	☐	AROUND_VALUE			
Number of border police agent	☐	☐	☐	☐				

Criminal record — WEIGHT / 142.85 — Add Qt

Text	Bg	Qt	Sc	V.	Direction	Weight		
Budget for justice	☐	☐	☐	☐	AROUND_VALUE			
Number of agent for justice	☐	☐	☐	☐	AROUND_VALUE			

Subjective Data from field — WEIGHT / 142.85 — Add Qt

Text	Bg	Qt	Sc	V.	Direction	Weight		
Number of field agents	☐	☐	☐	☐				

Criminals Association — WEIGHT / 142.85 — Add Qt

Text	Bg	Qt	Sc	V.	Direction	Weight		
Budget for crime association fight	☐	☐	☐	☐	AROUND_VALUE			
Number of agent for crime association	☐	☐	☐	☐	AROUND_VALUE			

Financial — WEIGHT / 142.85 — Add Qt

Text	Bg	Qt	Sc	V.	Direction	Weight		
number of agents dedicated to economic crime	☐	☐	☐	☐	AROUND_VALUE			

In the realm of public administration and policy analysis, it is imperative that the components of results and means closely align with the overarching goals of the General Review of Public Policies, aimed at enhancing state efficiency. This alignment involves a comprehensive analysis of the missions and actions of both the state and local governments, followed by the development and implementation of structural reform scenarios. The primary objectives of these reforms include state modernization, reduction of public expenditures, and the improvement of public policies.

To ensure the effectiveness and accountability of these reforms, it is crucial that budgetary indicators are directly reflected in the state's accounting practices. This integration facilitates a transparent and measurable evaluation of the financial impacts of public policies, enabling a clearer assessment of efficiency gains or losses. Such an approach not only promotes fiscal responsibility but also ensures that public resources are allocated in a manner that maximizes social welfare.

Structural Reform Scenarios: the implementation of structural reforms is a complex process that requires careful planning and execution. These reforms may encompass a wide range of measures, including organizational restructuring, the intro-duction of new governance models, and the optimization of resource allocation. By closely examining the functions and effectiveness of various state and local government activities, policymakers can identify areas where efficiencies can be achieved, thereby contributing to the overall goals of reducing public spending and enhancing service delivery.

State Modernization and Public Expenditure Reduction: the drive towards state modernization and public expenditure reduction is a critical component of the General Review of Public Policies. This involves not only cutting unnecessary costs but also rethinking and redesigning public services to better meet the needs of citizens. The use of technology, for example, can play a significant role in streamlining processes and improving accessibility, leading to more efficient and cost-effective service provision.

Improvement of Public Policies: the ultimate aim of aligning results and means with the review of public policies is to enhance the quality and effectiveness of public policies themselves. This requires a rigorous analysis of existing policies, identification of best practices, and the implementation of evidence-based reforms. By doing so, governments can ensure that policies are not only efficient in terms of resource use but also effective in achieving their intended outcomes.

Budgetary Indicators and State Accounting: the correspondence between budgetary indicators and state accounting is fundamental to the transparency and accountability of public financial management. By ensuring that budgetary allocations and expenditures are accurately reflected in the state's financial records, policymakers and the public can have a clear understanding of how resources are being used. This transparency is essential for building trust in public institutions and for enabling informed debate about the allocation of public resources.

The integration of results and means with the objectives of the General Review of Public Policies represents a critical strategy for enhancing the efficiency and effectiveness of public administration. Through the careful analysis of state functions, the implementation of structural reforms, and the rigorous evaluation of policy outcomes, governments can achieve significant improvements in state modernization, fiscal responsibility, and the quality of public services.

The process of adapting the model post-installation is iterative, involving close collaboration with the client to iteratively refine and enhance the model's accuracy and relevance. This approach ensures that the analytics cartridge not only meets the immediate analytical needs of the client but also possesses the flexibility to evolve in response to changing conditions and emerging requirements.

In conclusion, the development and implementation of our foundational analytics cartridge are grounded in a philosophy of flexibility, collaboration, and continuous improvement. By starting with classic indicators and employing a rigorous gap analysis process, we can create highly customized solutions that deliver valuable insights and support data-driven decision-making across a wide range of contexts and industries.

Chapter 1.3: Homeland in Aitek: BigData

"Big data, the invisible becomes visible, turning shadows of threats into actionable insights "

In this chapter, we explore the capabilities and functionalities of the DataWizard, a pivotal module within the Aitek platform, which serves as a bridge between theoretical models and the vast, often chaotic world of data lakes. The DataWizard's primary function is to establish connections between a structured semantic model, designed according to Aitek's formal methodology, and the disparate, unstructured data residing in data lakes, which lack inherent structure or apparent links among the stored information.

Theoretical Framework and Semantic Structuring: the foundation of the DataWizard's functionality lies in its ability to interpret and apply theoretical models to real-world data. These models are not abstract constructs but are designed with a deep understanding of the semantics underlying the data they aim to process. Aitek's formal methodology provides a structured approach to model development, ensuring that each model is semantically rich and capable of capturing the nuances of the data it is intended to analyze. This semantic structuring is critical for transforming theoretical concepts into actionable insights that can be applied to the data within a lake.

Data Lake Integration: data lakes are repositories that store vast amounts of raw data in its native format until it is needed. While these lakes offer the advantage of storing diverse types of data, from structured to unstructured, they often lack the organization necessary to make this information easily accessible or usable. The DataWizard module addresses this challenge by providing the tools needed to navigate this unstructured environment, identifying relevant data points, and drawing connections between these points and the theoretical models developed within the Aitek framework.

The Aitek model, as described and stored within the Aitek Knowledge Builder, provides a comprehensive set of information necessary for executing a formal risk analysis, including the weighting of different factors. This model operates within a framework that identifies and interacts with data residing in a data lake, establishing connections based on the relevancy and applicability of the data to the modeled risk analysis. This interaction is categorized into three distinct scenarios:

CASE 1: AUTOMATIC CONNECTION ESTABLISHMENT

In scenarios where there is an existence of a direct correlation between an indicator and one or more pieces of data within the data lake, such indicators are automatically flagged as connectable. This automated flagging signifies that the system has identified a direct, actionable link between the model's theoretical constructs and the empirical data, facilitating an automated integration process that enhances the model's analytical capabilities by leveraging real-world data.

CASE 2: MANUAL DATA ENTRY AND INTEGRATION

There are instances where data must be manually inputted into the system, either through qualitative references or via a structured Order Entry form and its corresponding information system. In these cases, the engine generates and automatically transmits the newly integrated information to the data lake, transforming this scenario into a variant of Case 1. However, these indicators are distinctly flagged as manually connectable, indicating that human intervention was required to establish the connection between the theoretical model and the empirical data. This manual process allows for the incorporation of data not automatically identified by the system, ensuring a more comprehensive analysis.

CASE 3: FLAGGING AS NON-APPLICABLE (NA)

Indicators that cannot be correlated with any data within the data lake, or for which no relevant data exists, are flagged as NA (Non-Applicable). These indicators are excluded from the performance calculation but are included in the computation of the completeness index. This index, detailed in the chapter on engine settings, provides a measure of how exhaustive and comprehensive the data integration and analysis process is, taking into account the totality of relevant and available data.

The NA flagging thus serves an important function in maintaining the integrity of the analysis by ensuring that only applicable and relevant data influences the outcome.

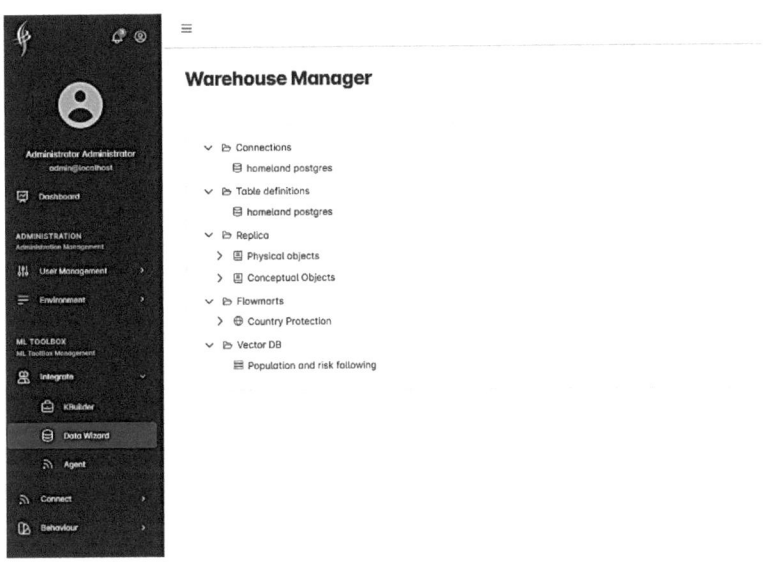

In the context of data management within the Aitek vector database, each case in the Aitek Model (Knowledge Builder) is assigned a specific sub-category flag, notably for real-time processing. When this flag is activated, it signifies that the corresponding indicator will undergo a specialized treatment in the Aitek vector database. Beyond its inclusion in the KnowledgeMart, the indicator's data elements are refreshed at the earliest opportunity within a designated zone of the database. This zone is characterized by a bijective link with the vector database, ensuring a one-to-one correspondence that enables the Aitek Query 360 to return the most recent value of the indicator (within a 3-15 minutes timeframe) rather than relying on the last update from the KnowledgeMart (which might have a 2-4 hour delay). This feature is particularly useful for tracking real-time data such as GPS location information. The operational mechanics of real-time processing within the vector database are elaborated upon in subsequent sections.

Real-Time Data Processing in Vector Databases: the integration of real-time data processing capabilities within a vector database architecture represents a significant advancement in data analytics. By assigning specific sub-category flags to indicators, the system can identify and prioritize data that require immediate refreshment. This mechanism ensures that critical information, such as dynamic GPS data, is updated and made available to users with minimal latency.

Bijective Link and Data Refreshment: the establishment of a bijective link between the real-time processing zone and the broader vector database is a key feature that facilitates the swift update of indicators. This one-to-one mapping ensures that each piece of data in the real-time zone has a corresponding element in the main database, allowing for seamless updates and data integrity. The refreshment of data elements within this specialized zone is managed with precision, ensuring that the most current data is always accessible for analysis.

Integration with Aitek Query 360: the specialized treatment of real-time data is closely integrated with the functionality of the Aitek Query 360 tool. By ensuring that the Query 360 accesses the most recent data values, users can obtain up-to-date information that reflects the current state of the indicators of interest. This capability is critical for applications where timely data is essential for decision-making, analysis, and operational efficiency.

Application to GPS Location Data: the utility of real-time data processing is exemplified in the tracking of GPS location information. In scenarios where the geographical position of assets or individuals is subject to rapid change, the ability to access and analyze up-to-the-minute location data can be invaluable. The real-time processing capabilities of the Aitek vector database ensure that such data is accurately captured and made available for immediate use.

The implementation of specific sub-category flags for real-time processing within the Aitek vector database significantly enhances the system's ability to manage and analyze time-sensitive data. By ensuring a bijective link between the real-time processing zone and the main database, and integrating this functionality with the Aitek Query 360 tool, the system provides users with access to the most current data. This capability is particularly beneficial for applications requiring immediate data updates, such as the tracking of GPS location information, underscoring the value of real-time data processing in modern data analytics frameworks.

Warehouse Manager

- ∨ 🗁 Connections
  - 🗄 homeland postgres
- ∨ 🗁 Table definitions
  - 🗄 homeland postgres
- ∨ 🗁 Replica
  - › 🗐 Physical objects
  - ∨ 🗐 Conceptual Objects
    - ∨ 🌐 Country Protection
      - ∨ 🛡 Homeland Security
        - ∨ 👤 Homeland supervisor
          - ∨ ⚑ Goods and people security
            - ∨ 🌐 Population and risk following
              - ∨ ❗ Population Risk Monitoring
                - › ⊕ Cross Border Data
                  - 🗓 Criminal record
                  - 🗓 Communication
                  - 🗓 Water/Electricity
                  - 🗓 Subjective Data from field
                  - 🗓 Criminals Association
                  - 🗓 Financial
- ∨ 🗁 Flowmarts

Edit Connection
Basic information

Name
homeland postgres

Description

Driver
org.postgresql.Driver

Url
jdbc:postgresql://engine-dev-db.postgres.database.azure.com/postgres

Username
postgres@engine-dev-db

Password
••••••••••••

In the initial phase of integrating and analyzing data within a data lake, one of the primary tasks involves the localization and connection to the datalake and its components. This process is facilitated through the utilization of standard drivers or a standard metadata extractor. The fundamental role of metadata in this context cannot be overstated; it serves as the backbone for organizing, accessing, and interpreting the vast amounts of unstructured data contained within a data lake. This chapter delves into the methodologies and technologies employed in the extraction and management of metadata, thereby enabling a structured approach to handling otherwise unstructured data repositories.

Metadata Extraction and Integration: the process of metadata extraction involves identifying and capturing essential information about the data files stored within the datalake. This metadata, once extracted, is typically organized into a Comma-Separated Values (CSV) format for ease of access and analysis. Examples of data that might be subject to this process include JPEG or PDF copies of passports, vehicle registration documents, and photographic identification. The conversion of these diverse data formats into a unified metadata framework is crucial for facilitating effective data management and retrieval processes.

Standard Drivers and Metadata Extractors: to connect to and interact with the datalake, standard drivers are employed. These drivers enable seamless access to the datalake's components, allowing for the efficient transfer and manipulation of data. In cases where the datalake's structure or the nature of its data requires specialized handling, the development of custom connectors or metadata extractors becomes necessary. These tools are tailored to address the unique challenges presented by specific data sources, ensuring that all relevant information can be accurately and efficiently extracted.

Custom Connectors and Reusability: the creation of custom connectors or metadata extractors is often driven by the need to accommodate data sources that cannot be effectively managed using standard tools. Once developed, if these custom solutions possess the potential for broader applicability, they may be incorporated into the standard toolkit. This approach not only enhances the flexibility and capability of the data management system but also contributes to the ongoing refinement and expansion of the standard methodologies employed for data integration and analysis within the datalake.

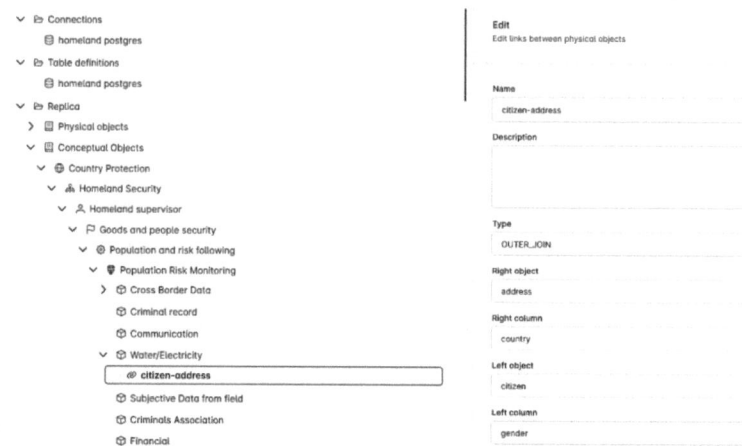

In the domain of data management and analysis, the initial step of engaging with a datalake involves the utilization of drivers to access and visualize its components, akin to navigating through an Excel spreadsheet or an SQL table. This chapter elucidates the process of opening drivers and systematically organizing the components within a datalake for efficient data analysis, highlighting the transformation of raw data into a structured and comprehensible format.

Visualization and Organization of Data Components: upon accessing the datalake via drivers, the data components are displayed in a manner that resembles an Excel spreadsheet or an SQL table, offering a visual representation of the data contained within. For instance, when connecting to a CSV connector in a directory containing ten files, or an SQL database with a hundred tables, the immediate task involves the visualization of these elements in an organized structure. This visual arrangement facilitates the subsequent steps of data management and analysis.

Renaming and Annotating Data Elements: a critical step in preparing the datalake for analysis involves the renaming of data elements to reflect their content accurately. For example, a file named "bxxxdhy" might be renamed to "Civil Status," providing a clear indication of the data it contains. Similarly, columns such as "col1" could be renamed to "Passport #" to specify the type of data they represent. Beyond mere renaming, the addition of comments to these elements is encouraged to provide context and enhance understanding for future reference. This practice of renaming and annotating ensures that the data within the datalake is not only accessible but also intelligible to analysts.

In the further development of data integration strategies within a datalake environment, an essential aspect involves the incorporation of information on standard data types for "replicat" processes, as well as the implementation of stan-dard and ad hoc data type converters, with a particular focus on dates and character sets. This chapter delves into the intricacies of managing data types in the "replicat" process, highlighting the significance of data type conversion and the critical role of metadata annotation in ensuring data integrity and usability. Additionally, we explore the functionality and implications of three specific checkboxes related to business and analytical entities, which play pivotal roles in the data "replicat" and integration process.

Standard and Ad Hoc Data Type Conversion: data type conversion is a fundamental process in the integration of data from diverse sources into a unified datalake architecture. Standard converters facilitate the seamless translation of common data types, ensuring consistency across replicate datasets. However, the complexity of data often necessitates the development of ad hoc converters, especially for handling specialized formats like dates and character sets. These customized converters address the unique challenges posed by specific data formats, ensuring that all data, regardless of its original type, is accurately represented and stored within the datalake.

Business and Analytical Entity Identification: the process of integrating data into a datalake requires careful consideration of the role and relevance of each data element. This consideration is operationalized through the use of three checkboxes: "Business Entity," "Analytical Entity," and "Include in Replication." The "Business Entity" checkbox indicates whether a data field represents a business concept that needs to be renamed according to the model's nomenclature and annotated with model-specific comments, potentially enriched with additional context. Similarly, the "Analytical Entity" checkbox identifies data fields that, while not necessarily business entities, are crucial for analytical processes and thus require similar treatment in terms of renaming and annotation. The "Include in Replicat" checkbox determines whether a data field should be replicated into the datalake, ensuring that only relevant data is included, thereby optimizing storage and processing efficiency.

Metadata Enrichment and Management: the management of metadata, particularly the enrichment of data fields with model-specific names and comments, is a critical aspect of data integration. This enrichment process not only enhances the understandability and accessibility of the data but also ensures that both business and analytical entities are clearly identified and appropriately managed within the datalake environment. By providing detailed metadata annotations, data scientists and analysts can navigate the complex landscape of integrated data with greater ease, facilitating more effective and insightful analysis.

Conclusion: the integration of diverse data sources into a datalake necessitates a sophisticated approach to data type conversion, entity identification, and metadata management. Through the judicious use of standard and ad hoc converters, alongside meticulous metadata annotation and entity identification, organizations can ensure that their datalake architecture not only accurately reflects the complexity of integrated data but also supports the advanced analytical and business processes that rely on this integrated data. This chapter has highlighted the key strategies and considerations involved in enhancing datalake functionality through effective data type management and entity identification, underscoring the importance of these processes in the broader context of data integration and analysis.

Creating a Data Dictionary for the Datalake: an essential component of organizing a datalake is the development of a data dictionary. This dictionary encompasses detailed information about each group of data, including the owning institution, contact person, email address, and telephone number. The creation of this dictionary during the initial phase of data organization plays a pivotal role in establishing a comprehensive reference resource that facilitates effective communication and collaboration among stakeholders involved in data analysis.

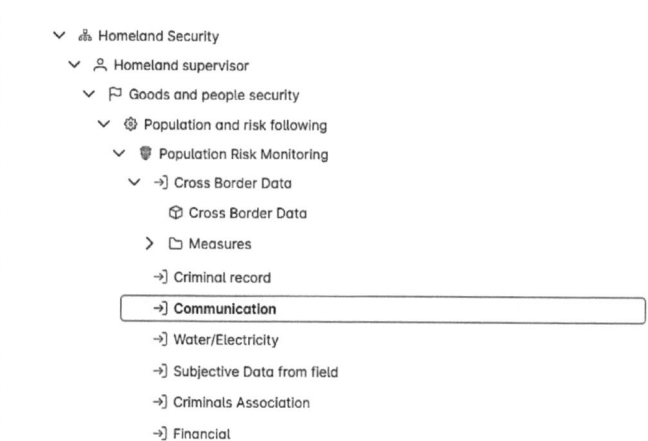

In this chapter, we delve into the construction and management of conceptual objects within a datalake, focusing on their role as aggregates composed of multiple, heterogeneously sourced elements that coalesce around a unified theme. The creation of these conceptual objects involves linking disparate data elements, potentially across the entirety or a subset of analytical entities, through either outer or inner join operations. This process culminates in the generation of an initialization (ini/json) file, which guides the preload program in its execution of tasks such as metadata extraction, data type unification, cleansing, and the creation of a pre-replicat dataset for each conceptual object.

Conceptual Object Construction: conceptual objects represent an advanced form of data aggregation, drawing together elements from varied sources within the datalake that pertain to a specific theme or subject matter. This aggregation process is instrumental in transcending the inherent heterogeneity of the datalake's sources, facilitating a thematic consolidation that enhances analytical utility and insight generation. The linkage of these data elements, whether through comprehensive inclusion or selective association of analytical entities, forms the structural basis of a conceptual object, embodying a distilled representation of thematic data.

Join Operations and Data Integration: the integration strategy for constructing conceptual objects employs join operations – either outer or inner joins – to establish relational connections between data elements. Outer joins are utilized to ensure that all relevant data, including those without direct counterparts in other datasets, are included in the conceptual object, thereby maximizing the breadth of thematic coverage. Inner joins, conversely, focus on the intersection of datasets, emphasizing data precision and relevance at the expense of breadth. The choice between these join types reflects a strategic decision in the balance between inclusivity and specificity in thematic aggregation.

Initialization File Generation and Preload Program Directive: the generation of an ini/json file as a product of the join operation serves a critical function, acting as a directive for the preload program. This file contains instructions for subsequent operations necessary for preparing the data for integration into conceptual objects. These operations include metadata extraction, which catalogs the properties and relationships of data elements; data type unification, ensuring consistency in data representation; data cleansing, which purifies the dataset of inaccuracies or irrelevancies; and the creation of a pre-replicat dataset, which assembles a ready-to-integrate collection of data for each conceptual object.

Metadata Management and Data Cleansing: essential to the process of conceptual object construction is the meticulous management of metadata and the cleansing of data. Metadata management involves documenting the origin, structure, and interrelationships of data elements within the conceptual object, providing a roadmap for navigation and analysis. Data cleansing purifies the dataset, removing errors, duplicates, and irrelevant entries to enhance the quality and reliability of the conceptual object.

In the architecture of data analytics within a datalake environment, the interconnection of conceptual objects forms the foundation of what can be referred to as a "flowmart," a term derived from the amalgamation of data flow and datamart concepts. This chapter explores the intricacies of creating a flowmart by joining conceptual objects, emphasizing the necessity to define aggregation rules and specify the segments of the business entity these rules apply to. This process is pivotal for ensuring that data analytics is both accurate and meaningful, providing actionable insights into business operations.

Conceptual Object Joining and Flowmart Construction: the process of joining conceptual objects to create a flowmart involves establishing relational links between different thematic aggregations of data. This step is crucial for constructing a comprehensive analytical model that reflects the multifaceted nature of business operations and insights. The flowmart thus created serves as an intermediary structure that facilitates complex analytical queries by providing a streamlined, topic-centric view of the data aggregated from the vast and diverse sources within the datalake.

Defining Aggregation Rules: central to the utility of the flowmart is the definition of specific aggregation rules for each measure. These rules determine how data from various conceptual objects are combined, summarized, or averaged to provide meaningful metrics. The establishment of these rules requires a deep understanding of the data's nature, the analytical objectives, and the implications of different aggregation methodologies on the outcome's interpretability and relevance.

Application to Business Entity Segments: aggregation rules are not universally applicable across all segments of a business entity; rather, they must be tailored to the particular characteristics and analytical needs of each segment. This tailored approach ensures that the aggregation process accurately reflects the unique operational dynamics and informational requirements of different areas within the business. For instance, aggregation rules applied to the sales domain may differ significantly from those relevant to supply chain management, reflecting the distinct data structures, metrics, and analytical goals of these business entities.

Operationalizing Flowmart for Analytical Queries: once the flowmart is established with clearly defined aggregation rules applied to specific business entity segments, it becomes an invaluable asset for conducting analytical queries. This operationalization involves utilizing the flowmart as a basis for extracting insights, identifying trends, and making data-driven decisions. The flowmart's structure enables analysts to navigate the complexities of the datalake's aggregated data efficiently, focusing on the specific measures and metrics that are most relevant to their analytical objectives.

The construction of a flowmart through the joining of conceptual objects and the careful definition of aggregation rules tailored to segments of the business entity represents a sophisticated approach to data analytics within a datalake environment. This methodology not only enhances the efficiency and efficacy of analytical queries but also ensures that the insights derived are deeply aligned with the specific informational needs and operational realities of the business. By providing a structured, topic-centric framework for data analysis, the flowmart significantly advances the capabilities of organizations to harness the full potential of their data assets for strategic decision-making.

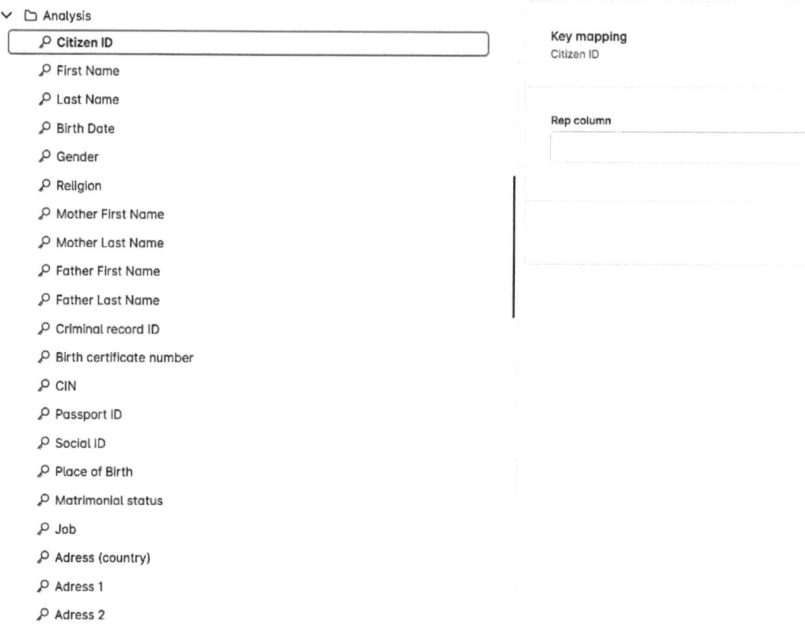

In the advanced stages of configuring a comprehensive data analysis framework within the Aitek ecosystem, a critical step involves the precise parameterization of analytical entities for inclusion in the Aitek Supervisor's Query 360. This chapter delves into the methodology and considerations essential for optimally setting up these entities, ensuring they are accurately represented and effectively utilized within the Query 360 environment. This setup is pivotal for enabling a holistic and multidimensional analysis, providing a 360-degree view of the data landscape from a supervisory perspective.

Parameterization of Analytical Entities: the process of parameterizing analytical entities involves defining and configuring the characteristics and data relationships of these entities to ensure their compatibility and effective function within the Query 360 tool. This includes specifying the data sources, attributes, and metrics that constitute each entity, as well as establishing the rules and logic for data aggregation, filtering, and presentation. The goal of this parameterization is to tailor the Query 360's functionality to meet the specific analytical needs and objectives of the supervisory framework, facilitating efficient and insightful data exploration and analysis.

Inclusion Criteria for Query 360: determining which analytical entities are included in the Query 360 involves a strategic evaluation of the entities' relevance to the supervisory objectives, their data quality and integrity, and their potential to contribute to a comprehensive understanding of the operational environment. This selection process is critical for ensuring that the Query 360 tool is populated with data that is not only relevant and actionable but also representative of the diverse aspects of the organization's operations and strategic interests.

Optimizing Analytical Entities for Comprehensive Analysis: Once selected, the analytical entities must be optimized for analysis within the Query 360 environment. This optimization includes fine-tuning the entities' data models to enhance their analytical utility, designing intuitive and informative visualizations, and integrating advanced analytical functions such as predictive modeling and trend analysis. The aim is to leverage the full capabilities of the Query 360 tool to extract maximum insights from the data, facilitating informed decision-making and strategic oversight.

Integration and Implementation: the final step in parameterizing analytical entities for the Query 360 involves their integration into the Aitek Supervisor's analytical framework. This includes the technical implementation of the entities within the Query 360 tool, testing to ensure accurate functionality and performance, and the establishment of protocols for ongoing data management and analysis. Effective integration ensures that the analytical entities function seamlessly within the Query 360 environment, providing a robust foundation for comprehensive data analysis.

The parameterization of analytical entities for inclusion in the Aitek Supervisor's Query 360 represents a critical component of setting up an effective data analysis framework. By carefully selecting, optimizing, and integrating these entities, organizations can harness the full power of the Query 360 tool to gain a 360-degree view of their data landscape. This holistic approach to data analysis enables supervisors to navigate complex data environments with ease, uncovering insights that drive strategic decision-making and operational excellence.

- City
- ZIP code
- Place of Workship
- Association
- Political party
- Bank Name
- Bank Country
- Account ID
- Transaction Type
- Transaction Date
- Transaction Descrition
- Bank Transaction Dest
- Entry Date
- Departure Date
- Transport Type
- Transport company
- Type of Trip
- Country Origin
- Country Destination
- Trip Type
- Date of offence/crime
- Type of offence/crime

- 🔍 Condemnation date
- 🔍 Nature and quantum of penalties
- 🔍 Electricity Invoice Date
- 🔍 Water Invoice Date
- 🔍 Operator
- 🔍 Phone source
- 🔍 Phone destination
- 🔍 Call Type
- 🔍 Call date
- 🔍 Vehicle purchase Date
- 🔍 Vehicle type
- 🔍 Licence plate ID
- 🔍 Insurance

∨ 📁 Business Entity
- 🔍 ZIP Code
- 🔍 Zone
- 🔍 Cluster HR
- 🔍 Cluster AI

In the advanced stages of configuring a comprehensive data analysis framework within the Aitek ecosystem, a critical step involves the precise parameterization of analytical entities for inclusion in the Aitek Supervisor's Query 360. This chapter delves into the methodology and considerations essential for optimally setting up these entities, ensuring they are accurately represented and effectively utilized within the Query 360 environment. This setup is pivotal for enabling a holistic and multidimensional analysis, providing a 360-degree view of the data landscape from a supervisory perspective.

Parameterization of Analytical Entities: the process of parameterizing analytical entities involves defining and configuring the characteristics and data relationships of these entities to ensure their compatibility and effective function within the Query 360 tool. This includes specifying the data sources, attributes, and metrics that constitute each entity, as well as establishing the rules and logic for data aggregation, filtering, and presentation. The goal of this parameterization is to tailor the Query 360's functionality to meet the specific analytical needs and objectives of the supervisory framework, facilitating efficient and insightful data exploration and analysis.

Inclusion Criteria for Query 360: determining which analytical entities are included in the Query 360 involves a strategic evaluation of the entities' relevance to the supervisory objectives, their data quality and integrity, and their potential to contribute to a comprehensive understanding of the operational environment. This selection process is critical for ensuring that the Query 360 tool is populated with data that is not only relevant and actionable but also representative of the diverse aspects of the organization's operations and strategic interests.

Optimizing Analytical Entities for Comprehensive Analysis: once selected, the analytical entities must be optimized for analysis within the Query 360 environment. This optimization includes fine-tuning the entities' data models to enhance their analytical utility, designing intuitive and informative visualizations, and integrating advanced analytical functions such as predictive modeling and trend analysis. The aim is to leverage the full capabilities of the Query 360 tool to extract maximum insights from the data, facilitating informed decision-making and strategic oversight.

Integration and Implementation: the final step in parameterizing analytical entities for the Query 360 involves their integration into the Aitek Supervisor's analytical frame-work. This includes the technical implementation of the entities within the Query 360 tool, testing to ensure accurate functionality and performance, and the establishment of protocols for ongoing data management and analysis. Effective integration ensures that the analytical entities function seamlessly within the Query 360 environment, providing a robust foundation for comprehensive data analysis.

The parameterization of analytical entities for inclusion in the Aitek Supervisor's Query 360 represents a critical component of setting up an effective data analysis framework. By carefully selecting, optimizing, and integrating these entities, organizations can harness the full power of the Query 360 tool to gain a 360-degree view of their data landscape. This holistic approach to data analysis enables supervisors to navigate complex data environments with ease, uncovering insights that drive strategic decision-making and operational excellence.

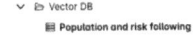

In the realm of data management and analysis, the generation of configuration files, notably ini/json files, plays a pivotal role in ensuring the accurate execution of processes within a vector database. This chapter explores the systematic creation and utilization of these configuration files, underscoring their significance in facilitating the seamless operation of various data processing stages. Specifically, the focus is on the preprocessing stage, real-time processing, and the loading phase, each of which contributes to the formation of a unified pre-replicat dataset (conceptual object), the propagation of real-time updates, and the creation of temporary replicas for advanced analysis, respectively.

Preprocessing Stage: the preprocessing stage involves the execution of the preload program, which is responsible for running metadata extractors and cleaners, as well as data extractors, to create a unified pre-replicat dataset, referred to as a conceptual object. The configuration files guide the preload program in identifying which data to process, how to clean and standardize it, and ultimately, how to amalgamate different data sources into a cohesive dataset. This stage is crucial for ensuring data quality and consistency before any further analysis is performed.

Real-Time Processing: in the context of real-time data processing, configuration files enable the propagation of updates to specific indicators directly to the repository on the server. This mechanism ensures that the most current data is available for analysis, reflecting changes and updates as they occur. The configuration files dictate the parameters for real-time updates, including the indicators to be updated, the frequency of updates, and the destination repository for these updates.

Loading Phase: the loading phase involves the creation of temporary replicas, utilizing artificial intelligence processes for clustering and the generation of agents by measure. This phase is instrumental in analyzing performance by nodes within the model, encompassing missions, business domains, processes, and activities. Furthermore, clustering is based on percentiles, allowing for the segmentation of data into meaningful groups for deeper analysis. The culmination of this phase is the creation of the KnowledgeMart for the "DO" cycle, along with the processes for creating KnowledgeMarts for the "PLAN," "CHECK," and "ACT" cycles.

The configuration files (ini/json) serve as the blueprint for each of these stages, specifying the operational parameters and ensuring that each process aligns with the overarching objectives of the data analysis framework. By meticulously defining the settings and instructions within these files, data scientists and analysts can harness the full potential of the vector database, facilitating a comprehensive approach to data analysis that spans preprocessing, real-time processing, and advanced analytical modeling.

The generation and implementation of configuration files are foundational to the effective management and analysis of data within a vector database environment. By guiding the execution of critical data processing stages, these files ensure that data is accurately cleaned, integrated, and analyzed, enabling the derivation of meaningful insights and the informed decision-making process. This chapter has highlighted the integral role of configuration files in enhancing the functionality and efficiency of data processing systems, demonstrating their indispensability in the pursuit of data-driven knowledge discovery.

Chapter 1.4: Homeland in Aitek: Config

"A well-set program is the lock; diligence in security is the key."

In this chapter, we delve into the configuration of peripheral devices and the implementation of Artificial Intelligence (AI) agents (Auto-ML or had hoc) on the server/engine side within the Aitek6 platform. This exploration is critical for understanding how devices interact with and are controlled by the central system, as well as how AI agents can enhance the platform's capabilities through intelligent analysis and decision-making processes. Importantly, the procedures and principles outlined here are applicable across all knowledge modules ("knowledge Cartridge") on the Aitek6 platform, ensuring a cohesive and standardized approach to system configuration and AI integration.

Peripheral Device Configuration: this process is predicated on the principle of connecting devices to the IoT Box, a foundational step in the architecture of modern data collection and analysis systems. This chapter delves into the methodologies and technologies involved in integrating various devices with the IoT Box, highlighting the pivotal role this connectivity plays in harnessing the power of the Internet of Things (IoT) for data-driven insights.

The IoT Box as a Connectivity Hub: the IoT Box serves as a critical hub for connecting a wide array of devices, from sensors and actuators to more complex machinery. This connectivity is essential for collecting the vast, diverse data streams that IoT devices generate. We explore the technical specifications of the IoT Box, including its compatibility with different device protocols, data transmission capabilities, and security features that ensure the integrity and privacy of the data collected.

Device Integration Principles: integrating devices with the IoT Box involves several key principles, including device recognition, data synchronization, and energy efficiency. Device recognition ensures that each connected device is correctly identified by the IoT Box, facilitating accurate data collection and analysis. Data synchronization addresses the challenge of managing real-time data streams from multiple devices, ensuring that the data is consistently and accurately aggregated. Energy efficiency is particularly crucial for battery-operated devices, requiring optimized communication protocols to extend device lifespan.

Configuring Devices for Optimal Data Collection: configuring devices for connection to the IoT Box involves setting parameters that dictate how and when data is collected and transmitted. This section outlines the processes for device configuration, including setting data sampling rates, transmission intervals, and thresholds for triggering alerts. The configuration process is essential for maximizing the quality and relevance of the data collected, ensuring that it meets the specific needs of the analysis being conducted.

Security and Privacy Considerations: As devices are connected to the IoT Box, security and privacy considerations become paramount. This part of the chapter addresses the strategies and technologies employed to secure device connections and protect the data collected from unauthorized access or tampering. This includes encryption protocols, secure device authentication methods, and data anonymization techniques, which are critical for maintaining the confidentiality and inte-grity of the data.

AI AGENT

The concept of an Agent, a specialized program designed to interface between a data source and output a vector. The Agent embodies a crucial component of data processing and analysis, facilitating the transformation of raw data into structured, analyzable formats. This exploration delves into the attributes of an Agent, including its author-ship, creation, versioning, conceptual and detailed descriptions, operational status, and implementation identifier. Additionally, we examine the operational dynamics of an Agent, such as its ability to be instantiated multiple times and the management of its lifecycle through maintenance, execution, and cessation, complemented by a comprehensive log of its operational history.

Agent Definition and Functionality: an Agent is defined as a program that inputs a data source and outputs a vector. This process involves the extraction, transformation, and loading (ETL) of data, rendering it suitable for further analysis. The functionality of an Agent is critical in data science and analytics, where the conversion of disparate data into a uniform format is essential for consistency and accuracy in analysis.

Agent Metadata: each Agent is accompanied by a set of metadata that details its origins, versions, and operational parameters. This metadata includes:

Author: the creator of the Agent.

Creation Date: the date on which the Agent was initially developed.

Version and Version Date: information detailing the iteration of the Agent and the date of that version.

Version Author: the individual responsible for the particular version of the Agent.

Conceptual and Detailed Description: a comprehensive explanation of the Agent's purpose, functionality, and operational methodology.

Status: the current operational state of the Agent, which can range from maintenance and running to stopped.

Implementation ID: a unique identifier that allows for the tracking and management of different instances of the Agent.

Operational Dynamics of an Agent: the Agent's design allows for multiple instances to be operational simultaneously, accommodating various states such as maintenance, active execution, and cessation. This multiplicity is critical for ensuring that data processing can continue uninterrupted, even as individual instances undergo maintenance or updates.

Lifecycle Management: agents are equipped with lifecycle management capabilities, allowing administrators to start, stop, and restart instances based on operational needs. This flexibility is vital for maintaining the continuity of data processing activities and for implementing updates or modifications to the Agent's programming without significant downtime.

Operational History: an integral feature of an Agent is its ability to log its operational history, including the origin of its execution, duration, and any events or errors that occurred. This historical log is crucial for troubleshooting, performance evaluation, and optimizing the Agent's future iterations.

We delve into the critical aspect of an Agent's physical deployment, specifically its installation across various Virtual Machines (VMs), and the categorization of Agents based on their functionality and origin. This exploration is instrumental in understanding the operational dynamics and the scope of tasks that Agents can perform within a data processing ecosystem. We categorize Agents into several types: AI Agents generated by the vector database (auto-ML), third-party AI Agents, metadata extractors, and basic robotic Agents that perform generic tasks. Each category plays a distinct role in the data analysis and management process, contributing to the system's overall functionality and efficiency.

Physical Deployment of Agents: the physical location where an Agent is installed, particularly the specific VMs, is a pivotal factor that influences its performance and accessibility. The distribution of Agents across VMs needs to be strategically planned to optimize resource utilization, ensure redundancy, and facilitate scalable deployment. This section discusses the considerations involved in deploying Agents on VMs, including load balancing, fault tolerance, and the integration with cloud services for enhanced flexibility.

AI Agents Generated by Auto-ML: AI Agents created by the vector database's auto-ML feature represent a significant advancement in automated data analysis. These Agents are designed to simplify complex data sets into more understandable formats, often employing graphical representations such as B-tree visualizations of training data. This "vulgarization" process makes intricate data structures accessible and comprehensible to users, enhancing the interpretability of analytical results.

Third-party AI Agents: AI Agents developed by external entities are required to adhere to the same operational standards as those generated by the auto-ML system. This ensures consistency in behavior and output, facilitating seamless integration within the data processing framework. The inclusion of third-party AI Agents allows for the incorporation of specialized analytical capabilities, expanding the system's range of functions and applications.

Metadata Extractors and Basic Robotic Agents: Metadata extractors and basic robotic Agents are tasked with performing a variety of generic functions, such as sending emails, executing tasks within applications (e.g., acknowledging an alarm, initiating an action plan, deleting a record, creating or reading a dashboard). These Agents form a standard library of robotic functions that can be expanded and customized according to specific operational needs. The flexibility and modularity of these Agents are crucial for automating routine tasks and integrating action plans within the data processing ecosystem.

Enrichment and Utilization of the Standard Robotic Library: The standard library of robotic Agents offers a foundation that can be enriched with additional functionalities over time. By leveraging this library, organizations can automate a wide array of tasks, from basic operational procedures to more complex analytical processes. This section outlines strategies for expanding the robotic library and integrating these Agents into comprehensive action plans, thereby enhancing the system's automation capabilities and operational efficiency.

The deployment and categorization of Agents within a data processing ecosystem play a vital role in enhancing the system's analytical and operational capabilities. From AI Agents that demystify complex data structures to basic robotic Agents that automate routine tasks, the diversity and functionality of these Agents contribute significantly to the system's effectiveness. By strategically deploying Agents across VMs and leveraging the synergies between different types of Agents, organizations can achieve a highly efficient, scalable, and flexible data analysis and management frame-work. This chapter has provided a comprehensive overview of the roles, deployment strategies, and potential enhancements of Agents, highlighting their importance in the broader con-text of data science and technology.

DEVICE

In this segment, we examine the role and functionality of devices within the Aitek ecosystem, focusing specifically on both analog and digital sensors capable of exchanging information streams with the Aitek engine via an IoT Box. This setup encapsulates the complexities of integration and facilitates the decentralization of processing tasks. The discussion herein elaborates on the operational principles of these devices, their integration with the IoT Box, and the resultant impact on the Aitek system's efficiency and scalability.

Devices in the Aitek Ecosystem: Devices, encompassing both analog and digital sensors, serve as the primary interface for data collection in the Aitek ecosystem. These devices are engineered to detect, measure, and transmit data about various physical conditions and environmental parameters. The ability of these devices to communicate with the Aitek engine via an IoT Box is pivotal for transforming raw sensory data into actionable insights.

Integration via IoT Box: the IoT Box plays a central role in simplifying the integration of devices within the Aitek ecosystem. It acts as an intermediary that not only facilitates the communication between sensors and the Aitek engine but also encapsulates the intricacies involved in this process. By providing a unified platform for device connectivity, the IoT Box enhances the system's ability to assimilate and process data from a diverse array of sources.

Decentralization of Processing: one of the significant advantages of utilizing the IoT Box for device integration is the decentralization of processing tasks. By offloading certain computational duties to the IoT Box, the system can distribute processing loads more evenly across the network. This decentralization is crucial for improving the system's overall performance, reducing latency in data processing, and enhancing the scalability of the Aitek ecosystem.

Operational Efficiency and Scalability: The integration and decentralization strategies employed in the Aitek ecosystem contribute substantially to its operational efficiency and scalability. Devices, through their communication with the IoT Box, enable the system to collect and process a vast amount of data in real-time. The decentralization of processing tasks further ensures that the system can handle increasing data volumes without compromising on performance or speed.

We delve into the nuanced process of metadata management within the Internet of Things (IoT) ecosystem, particularly focusing on the transformation and transmission of metadata through the IoT Box. This exploration is divided into two primary segments: the description of metadata post-translation within the IoT Box, and the metadata that needs to be sent prior to translation by the IoT Box. Understanding these processes is pivotal for ensuring the integrity, accuracy, and utility of metadata as it navigates through the IoT system, facilitating effective communication between devices and the central data processing infrastructure.

Metadata Post-Translation in the IoT Box: The IoT Box acts as a critical node in the IoT ecosystem, not only facilitating data communication but also transforming metadata from its raw, device-specific format into a standardized form suitable for integration into the broader data system. Post-translation metadata within the IoT Box includes standardized identifiers, timestamps, and data types, which are harmonized to ensure consistency across diverse data sources. This section explores the mechanisms through which the IoT Box processes and standardizes metadata, including the conversion protocols and the criteria used to maintain data fidelity and coherence.

Pre-Translation Metadata Requirements: Before metadata undergoes transformation within the IoT Box, it must be prepared and sent in a format that retains essential information while being adaptable for standardization. Pre-translation metadata typically encompasses device-specific identifiers, original timestamps, and proprietary data formats. This segment discusses the preparation and transmission of metadata to the IoT Box, emphasizing the importance of maintaining data integrity and the methodologies for encapsulating device-specific nuances in the metadata.

Metadata Transformation Process: the transformation of metadata by the IoT Box is a multifaceted process that involves data parsing, mapping to standard schemas, and the application of data integrity checks. This process ensures that once metadata is integrated into the central data system, it remains meaningful, accurate, and consistent with the system's analytical frameworks. The intricacies of the metadata transformation process are examined, including the algorithms and data structures employed to facilitate efficient and error-free translation.

Ensuring Metadata Integrity and Usability: the integrity and usability of metadata post-translation are of paramount importance for the effective functioning of the IoT ecosystem. This section outlines the strategies and technologies implemented within the IoT Box to verify metadata accuracy, including error detection mechanisms, validation against standard schemas, and the reconciliation of discrepancies. The role of metadata in enhancing data discoverability, interoperability, and analysis within the IoT system is also discussed, highlighting its significance in driving insights and decision-making.

The management and transformation of metadata within the IoT Box represent critical components of the data processing pipeline in the IoT ecosystem. By meticulously detailing the processes involved in preparing metadata for translation and ensuring its integrity post-translation, this chapter underscores the foundational role of metadata in bridging the gap between diverse IoT devices and the centralized data analytics infrastructure. Through effective metadata management, the IoT Box enhances the cohesion, reliability, and analytical value of data within the IoT ecosystem, enabling sophisticated analyses and insights that drive innovation and efficiency.

The integration of analog and digital sensors through the IoT Box into the Aitek ecosystem represents a sophisticated approach to data collection and processing. This arrangement not only simplifies the complexities associated with device integration but also facilitates the decentralization of processing, thereby enhancing the system's efficiency and scalability. By leveraging the capabilities of these devices and the IoT Box, the Aitek system is well-positioned to handle the demands of modern data analytics, making it an invaluable tool for extracting meaningful insights from the physical world.

IOT BOX

In this chapter, we explore the architectural framework of the IoT Box, a pivotal component in the Internet of Things (IoT) ecosystem, structured conceptually into three primary layers: acquisition, processing, and communication and management. This tri-layered architecture facilitates the seamless transition of data from its point of collection through devices to its eventual integration into the Aitek vector database. The focus here is on delineating the functionalities and interactions between these layers, particularly emphasizing the role of buffer management in pre-replication data handling and the conceptualization of data as it moves through the IoT Box to the datalake/vectorial database of Aitek.

Acquisition Layer: the acquisition layer serves as the entry point for data into the IoT Box, handling the initial collection of data from one to "n" devices. This layer is responsible for aggregating the data emanating from various sources, each contributing to the cumulative data description that forms the basis of the pre-replicated data of the IoT Box. The diversity and variability of these data sources necessitate a robust and flexible approach to data acquisition, ensuring that all relevant data attributes are accurately captured and consolidated.

Processing Layer: following acquisition, the data enters the processing layer, where it undergoes various transformations to refine and prepare it for integration into the datalake or vectorial database. This stage is critical for ensuring data quality and consistency, involving operations such as filtering, normalization, and enrichment. The processing layer acts on the data based on predefined rules and algorithms, shaping it into a form that aligns with the analytical models and structures of the Aitek vector database.

Communication and Management Layer: the final layer focuses on the communication and management aspects, including the crucial process of buffering pre-replicated data. This buffering mechanism plays a key role in managing data flow between the IoT Box and the datalake/vectorial database, ensuring that data is transmitted efficiently and without loss. Additionally, this layer oversees the synchronization and security of data transmission, maintaining the integrity and confidentiality of the data as it moves to its final destination.

Integration into the Aitek Vector Database: The culmination of the data's journey through the IoT Box is its integration into the Aitek vector database, where it can be modeled as a conceptual object within the "DO" phase of database creation. This conceptualization allows for the nuanced representation of data, facilitating its analysis and application within the broader context of the IoT ecosystem's analytical needs.

The IoT Box's architecture, characterized by its three-layered structure, plays an indispensable role in the data lifecycle within the IoT ecosystem. From the initial acquisition of data from diverse devices to its processing and eventual communication to the Aitek vector database, each layer of the IoT Box contributes to the efficient and secure handling of data. Through this structured approach, the IoT Box not only simplifies the complexities associated with data integration but also enhances the potential for deriving actionable insights from the vast data landscapes typical of IoT environments.

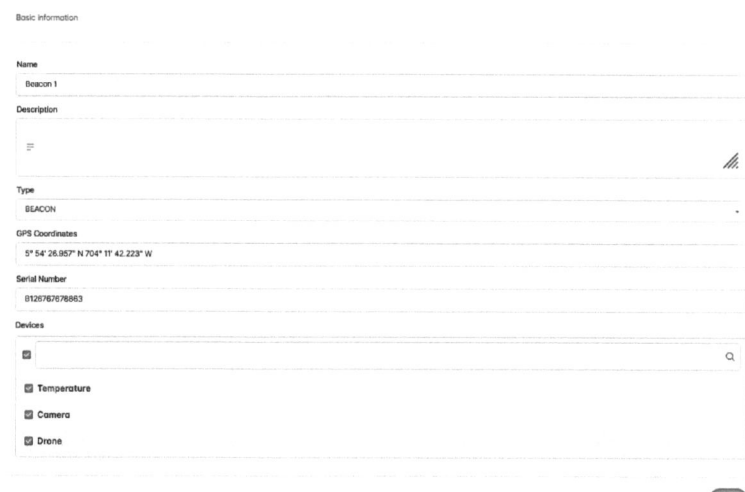

In the realm of Internet of Things (IoT) technologies, the IoT Box represents a crucial component for data acquisition and device management. This chapter delves into the essential information required for the configuration of each IoT Box, including its serial number, GPS positioning, and a unique certificate. The focus is on understanding the security measures, synchronization processes, and the association of devices to the IoT Box, culminating in the generation of a prereplicated dataset associated with the device.

Serial Number and Security: the serial number of an IoT Box is a critical piece of information, serving as a unique identifier for each unit. While this number is stored in plaintext on the server for administrative and tracking purposes, it is encrypted on the IoT Box itself to maintain security and prevent unauthorized access. This dual approach to handling the serial number exemplifies the balance between accessibility for system administrators and the need for security within the IoT ecosystem.

GPS Positioning and Device Association: the inclusion of GPS positioning data for each IoT Box facilitates precise location tracking, which is essential for a range of applications from logistics and fleet management to environmental monitoring. This geolocation data, coupled with the IoT Box's capabilities, allows for the dynamic association of devices based on geographical parameters, enhancing the system's responsiveness and data relevance.

Certificate Generation and Synchronization: a unique certificate, exemplified by a format such as: "IoT11767!@KjLUM--!!ZtTrx>" is generated for each IoT Box. This certificate is visible for a brief window of 60 seconds during the physical installation and synchronization of the IoT Box. This short visibility window is a security measure designed to protect the integrity of the synchronization process, ensuring that only authorized personnel can complete the installation and configuration of the IoT Box. The generation and management of these certificates are crucial for establishing a secure communication channel between the IoT Box and the central server.

Pre-Replicated Dataset Generation: the final step in the configuration process involves the generation of a pre-replicated dataset associated with the IoT Box. This dataset serves as an intermediary data structure, facilitating the preliminary aggregation and processing of data from connected devices before its integration into the central data repository. The generation of this pre-replicated dataset is a pivotal process that ensures data collected by the IoT Box is accurately reflected and available for analysis within the broader data system.

The configuration and management of IoT Boxes within the IoT ecosystem encompass several critical processes, from the secure handling of serial numbers and the generation of unique certificates to the precise tracking of GPS positioning and the association of devices. Each step in this process not only enhances the security and efficiency of data collection but also ensures that the data is primed for analysis, underpinning the IoT Box's role as a fundamental component in the collection, processing, and analysis of IoT data. Through these mechanisms, the IoT Box facilitates a robust, secure, and efficient framework for leveraging IoT technologies in data-driven applications.

CLUSTER

we delve into the intricacies of clustering techniques applied within the realm of data analytics, focusing on the categorization of clusters based on indicator families across all analytical entities, and the comprehensive clustering across the entirety of the KnowledgeMart. These methodologies are pivotal for assessing performance, identifying outliers within indices/indicators, and facilitating the automated or manual categorization of data through unsupervised classification algorithms. The discussion herein aims to elucidate the processes involved in creating these clusters, their application in data analysis, and the implications for enhancing data-driven insights.

Clustering by Indicator Families: clustering based on families of indicators involves grouping data points according to shared characteristics or metrics within specific sets of analytical entities. This approach allows for the nuanced evaluation of performance and the identification of outliers (outlayers) within specific indices or indicators. Such clustering not only aids in pinpointing areas of exceptional performance or concern within a dataset but also enhances the understanding of relationships and patterns among the indicators. This section will explore the methodologies employed to calculate these clusters, including the selection of relevant indicators and the application of clustering algorithms tailored to the nuances of indicator families.

Comprehensive Clustering in the KnowledgeMart: beyond the specific clustering by indicator families, there exists an approach to cluster analysis that encompasses the entirety of the KnowledgeMart. This broader clustering can be executed manually or automatically, leveraging unsupervised classification algorithms to organize and categorize the data. Unsupervised learning algorithms, such as k-means, hierarchical clustering, and DBSCAN, are instrumental in discerning inherent groupings within the data without predefined labels or categories. This segment will delve into the selection and application of these algorithms, the criteria for defining clusters, and the process of cataloging the resultant groupings within the KnowledgeMart.

Cataloging and Utilization of Clusters: the cataloging of clusters, whether derived from indicator families or the comprehensive KnowledgeMart, is a critical step in making the clustered data actionable. Cataloged clusters are systematically documented and made accessible for analysis, enabling researchers and data analysts to easily retrieve and examine specific groupings of interest. This organization facilitates deeper insights into the data, supporting targeted analysis and decision-making processes. The techniques and tools used for cataloging, as well as the integration of these clusters into analytical workflows, will be discussed.

Implications for Data Analysis and Insights: the strategic application of clustering techniques significantly impacts the ability to derive meaningful insights from data. By effectively grouping data points based on shared characteristics or through holistic analysis, researchers can uncover patterns, trends, and anomalies that might not be apparent through other analytical methods. This chapter will highlight the implications of these clustering techniques for data analysis, including their role in enhancing data interpretability, supporting hypothesis testing, and guiding strategic decision-making.

The use of clustering techniques to organize and analyze data within the KnowledgeMart presents a powerful tool for uncovering insights and understanding complex datasets. Whether focusing on specific families of indicators or employing a comprehensive approach across the Knowledge-Mart, the strategic application of these methods enhances the depth and breadth of data analysis. Through careful calculation, cataloging, and utilization of clusters, data scientists can unlock new avenues of inquiry and drive informed decisions based on a nuanced understanding of the data landscape.

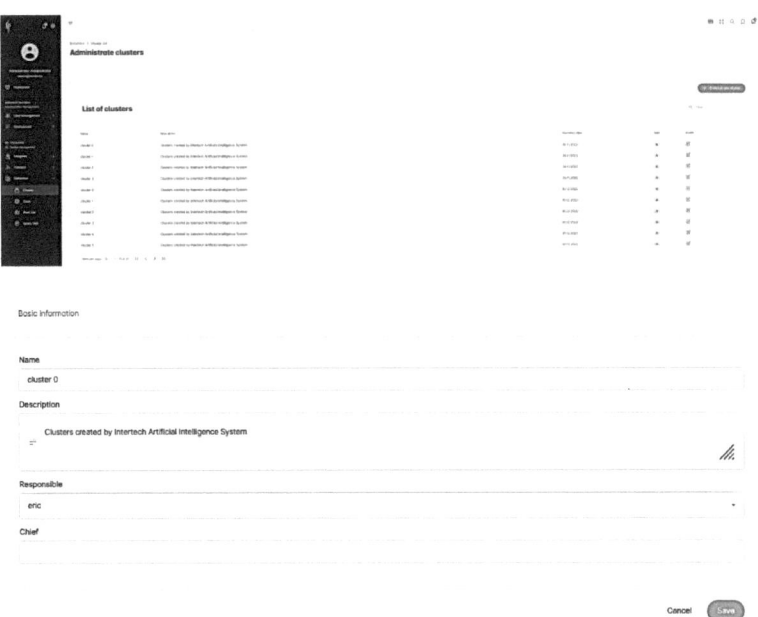

Beyond the conventional information such as names and sources, whether an AI agent from Aitek or a human user of the platform, and comments, it is also essential to designate a responsible party. This individual is an Aitek platform user who must oversee the network independent of the "Aitek zone" geographical area where the cluster is distributed, because on a territory a clusteur is distributed with different densities on several subparts of this territory.

With "chief" tag, being determined either through computation or manual input: which individual or group of individuals (cluster being in this case a sub-cluster) with a likelihood index. Within the network cluster, if a member does not communicate with others, they are assigned a "Fit". A citizen possessing this "profile" who engages with other members is categorized by the AI as a "member". Conversely, a citizen without the profile but who still interacts (financially, through telecommunications, or by providing accommodation) is classified as a "sympathizer" by Aitek's AI.

This chapter delves into the layered approach to data classification within the Aitek ecosystem, highlighting the nuanced methodology employed to differentiate between users based on their interaction patterns and profiles. This differentiation is pivotal for understanding the dynamics within a network and for tailoring the platform's functionality to meet the diverse needs of its user base.

Designation of Responsibility and Leadership: the assignment of responsible individuals and leaders within the Aitek platform network is a critical process that ensures effective oversight and management. The mechanism for identifying these roles—whether through AI calculation or manual designation—reflects the platform's flexibility in adapting to various operational scenarios. This section explores the criteria and algorithms used to assign these roles, emphasizing the importance of leadership in network coherence and efficiency.

Classification of Network Members: the classification system employed by Aitek's AI distinguishes between different types of network participants: profiles, members, and sympathizers. This classification is based on the extent and nature of their interactions within the network. Profiles are assigned to individuals with minimal or no communication with other members, serving as a basic identifier. Members are those who actively engage with the network, exhibiting patterns of communication that integrate them more deeply into the network's fabric. Sympathizers, while not directly fitting the member profile, still interact with the network in significant ways, such as through financial support or other forms of aid.

Impact of AI Classification on Network Analysis: the AI-driven classification system enhances the platform's analytical capabilities, enabling a more granular understanding of network dynamics. By categorizing individuals based on their interaction patterns, the AI facilitates targeted interventions and the development of customized strategies for network engagement and management. This section discusses the implications of AI classification for network analysis, including the potential for predictive modeling and behavior analysis.

The sophisticated classification system within the Aitek platform, powered by AI, plays a crucial role in dissecting and understanding the complex web of interactions among network participants. By categorizing individuals as profiles, members, or sympathizers based on their engagement levels, Aitek's AI provides valuable insights into the network's structure and dynamics. This layered approach to data classification not only enhances the platform's functionality but also opens new avenues for research and application in network analysis and management.

ZONE

Within the Aitek platform, the concept of a "zone" is universally applied across all knowledge modules and represents a geographic delineation on a specified territory, defined by simple geometric shapes such as rectangles or circles. This chapter aims to dissect the significance of zone demarcation within the Aitek platform, examining how these geographically defined areas facilitate targeted data analysis and operational efficiency within diverse knowledge domains. The discussion will explore the methodology for zone determination, the application of these zones within the platform's analytical framework, and the impact of this spatial structuring on data management and decision-making processes.

Methodology for Zone Determination: the process of zone determination within the Aitek platform involves selecting specific geographic territories and defining their boundaries using simple geometric shapes. This section delves into the criteria and tools used for zone delineation, including Geographic Information System (GIS) technologies and spatial analysis algorithms. The choice of rectangles or circles as the primary shapes for zone definition is discussed in terms of ease of implementation, computational efficiency, and applicability to a wide range of scenarios.

Application of Zones in Analytical Frameworks: once defined, these zones serve as fundamental units of analysis within the Aitek platform's various knowledge modules. Zones enable the platform to segment data geographically, allowing for localized analysis that can uncover region-specific insights and patterns. This part of the chapter examines how zones are utilized across different knowledge modules, from environmental monitoring to urban planning and security analysis, highlighting their versatility and utility in enhancing the platform's analytical capabilities.

Impact of Spatial Structuring on Data Management: The implementation of zones as a spatial structuring mechanism significantly influences the management and interpretation of data within the Aitek platform. By organizing data according to predefined geographic areas, the platform can optimize data storage, retrieval, and analysis processes. This section explores the benefits of spatial structuring, including improved data accessibility, enhanced analytical precision, and the facilitation of scalable data architectures.

Decision-Making and Operational Efficiency: the delineation of zones within the Aitek platform plays a pivotal role in supporting informed decision-making and operational efficiency. Geographic zones enable decision-makers to focus on specific areas of interest, tailoring strategies and interventions to the unique characteristics and needs of each zone. The chapter concludes by discussing the implications of zone-based analysis for operational planning, resource allocation, and policy formulation, underscoring the value of geographic specificity in achieving targeted and effective outcomes.

The concept of zones within the Aitek platform exemplifies the integration of geographic intelligence into data analysis and decision-making processes. By demarcating territories usi simple geometric shapes and applying these zones across various knowledge modules, the Aitek platform harnesses the power of spatial data to unlock region-specific insights and enhance operational effectiveness. This chapter has illuminated the methodologies, applications, and impacts of zone determination, affirming the critical role of geographic delineation in the realm of data-driven analysis and action.

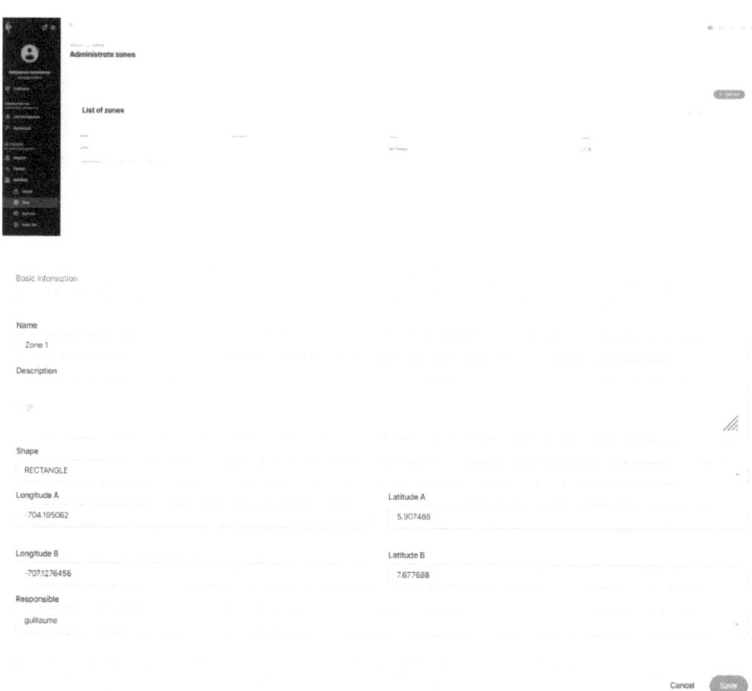

we delve into the critical role of the Zone Manager within the operational framework, emphasizing the importance of this position not merely for oversight purposes but also for its necessity in maintaining close ties with on-the-ground realities. The Zone Manager's responsibilities extend beyond mere supervision; they encompass a deep understanding of the local landscape, including direct knowledge of security forces such as police, firefighters, and the National Guard, as well as key local stakeholders like merchants, healthcare providers, and financial actors. This understanding incorporates both the strengths and weaknesses, as well as the actual capabilities of these entities, providing a comprehensive awareness of the zone's operational environment. This section explores the significance of the Zone Manager's role, particularly in response to alarms within a cluster, detailing how, while the action plan may be overseen by the cluster's supervisor, it is the Zone Manager who executes the necessary actions within their designated area.

Integration with Local Security Forces: the Zone Manager's relationship with local security forces is paramount for effective incident response and crisis management. This subsection examines the strategies for building and maintaining these critical relationships, ensuring that when an alarm is raised within a cluster, the Zone Manager can swiftly mobilize the necessary security responses tailored to the zone's specific needs and challenges.

Engagement with Community and Economic Stakeholders: beyond security considerations, the Zone Manager's engagement with local merchants, healthcare professionals, and financial actors is crucial for a holistic understanding of the zone's operational landscape. This engagement aids in identifying potential vulnerabilities and resources, enabling a comprehensive approach to planning and action. This part of the chapter discusses methods for cultivating these relationships and integrating stakeholder insights into operational planning and crisis response.

Understanding of Local Challenges and Capabilities: a deep understanding of the local challenges and capabilities within a zone allows the Zone Manager to make informed decisions and take effective actions in response to incidents. This understanding is not limited to security concerns but encompasses economic, health, and social factors that influence the zone's overall resilience. This section details the importance of this comprehensive awareness and the approaches for its acquisition and application in operational contexts.

Operational Response to Alarms: in the event of an alarm within a cluster, the delineation of responsibilities between the cluster's supervisor and the Zone Manager becomes crucial. While the supervisor may oversee the broader action plan, it is the Zone Manager who executes the response within their zone, leveraging their local knowledge and relationships. This subsection explores the dynamics of this response mechanism, highlighting the Zone Manager's role in ensuring an effective, localized reaction to incidents.

The role of the Zone Manager is indispensable within the operational framework, bridging the gap between high-level oversight and ground-level realities. Through their deep local knowledge and relationships across security, economic, and community stakeholders, Zone Managers are uniquely positioned to respond effectively to incidents within their zones. This chapter has highlighted the multifaceted responsibilities of the Zone Manager, emphasizing the critical nature of their role in achieving operational efficiency and resilience in response to challenges and alarms.

BURN LIST

we explore the concept of a "burn list" within the context of data privacy and security in the Aitek platform's vector database system. The burn list functions as a mechanism to obscure specific pieces of sensitive information that are returned by queries made through the Aitek Query 360 API.

Access to the obscured information on the burn list is restricted and can only be granted through specific levels of accreditation (Aitek roles), ensuring that sensitive data is only visible to authorized personnel. This protective measure is primarily aimed at safeguarding the privacy of influential members or security personnel and their families within a country, limiting exposure of critical information such as real-time locations, addresses, vehicle registration plates, banking details, telephone numbers, etc. In the event of queries, alarms, or detected anomalies, only the individual's identity number, name, and surname are made visible. This section delves into the rationale, implementation, and implications of the burn list for data security and privacy within the Aitek platform.

Rationale Behind the Burn List: the burn list addresses the crucial need for privacy and security for certain individuals and their families by selectively obscuring sensitive information from general query results. This subsection discusses the importance of balancing data accessibility with privacy concerns, especially in scenarios involving national security or the protection of high-profile individuals.

Implementation of the Burn List: implementing a burn list within a vector database system involves the designation of specific data fields as sensitive and subject to obscuration. This part of the chapter examines the technical mechanisms by which the Aitek platform manages the burn list, including the process for marking data, the role-based access control system that governs visibility, and the integration of these controls within the platform's API.

Accreditation and Access Control: access to the information obscured by the burn list is tightly controlled through a system of accreditation, with specific Aitek roles designated as having the authority to view such sensitive data. This section explores the accreditation levels required to access burn list information, the assignment of roles within the Aitek platform, and the measures in place to ensure that access rights are appropriately granted and managed.

Protective Measures for Sensitive Information: The burn list serves as a critical protective measure for sensitive personal information within the Aitek platform. By limiting the visibility of information such as real-time locations and contact details, the platform enhances the security and privacy of individuals deemed at risk. This subsection details the types of information protected by the burn list and the implications of these protections for individual privacy and security.

The implementation of a burn list within the Aitek platform's vector database system represents a sophisticated approach to managing data privacy and security. By selectively obscuring sensitive information and restricting access through a system of accreditation, the platform addresses critical privacy concerns while maintaining operational functionality. This chapter has highlighted the significance of the burn list in safeguarding the privacy of influential and security-sensitive individuals, underscoring its importance in the broader context of data security and privacy management.

QUERY 360 SETUP

In configuring the Query 360 feature of the Aitel platform, regardless of the specific knowledge module being utilized, a critical step involves selecting from the vector database's KnowledgeMart the key analytical fields that will serve as search criteria within the Aitek supervisor interface. This process necessitates a careful determination of which criteria will be mandatory for searches, ensuring that queries are both precise and relevant. Subsequently, it is essential to decide which pieces of information should be returned by the query to the Aitek supervisor. Naturally, these decisions have significant implications for the configuration of the query buffers and the response times during query executions. This chapter aims to dissect the configuration process of the Query 360, highlighting the strategic selection of search criteria and returned information, and exploring the impact of these choices on system performance and user experience.

Selection of Search Criteria: the initial step in configuring Query 360 involves the careful selection of key fields from the KnowledgeMart that will be used as criteria for search queries. This section delves into the methodologies for identifying the most relevant and informative criteria, considering factors such as data completeness, relevance to user needs, and potential for generating actionable insights. The process for designating certain criteria as mandatory for query execution is also discussed, emphasizing the balance between query specificity and flexibility.

Determining Returned Information: once search criteria have been established, the next step is to decide which pieces of information the Query 360 should return in response to user queries. This decision is crucial for ensuring that the query results are meaningful and actionable for the user. This part of the chapter explores the criteria for selecting returned information, including data relevance, the potential for overload, and the importance of data visualization in enhancing interpretability.

Impact on Query Buffer Configuration: the choices made regarding search criteria and returned information directly influence the configuration of the query buffers. These buffers play a key role in managing data flow and query processing, affecting the system's overall performance and response times. This section examines the technical aspects of query buffer configuration, including size, data management strategies, and optimization techniques to ensure efficient query processing.

Response Times During Query Executions: the configuration decisions also impact the response times experienced by users during query executions. Faster response times are critical for a positive user experience, especially in decision-critical applications. This part of the chapter assesses the factors that influence response times, including hardware capabilities, network conditions, and data complexity, and discusses strategies for minimizing delays and enhancing system responsiveness.

The configuration of the Query 360 within the Aitel platform is a complex process that requires careful consideration of various factors, from the selection of search criteria and returned information to the technical configuration of query buffers and optimization for quick response times. By strategically navigating these decisions, the platform can provide a powerful, efficient, and user-friendly querying interface that leverages the full potential of the KnowledgeMart and vector database. This chapter has provided a comprehensive overview of the configuration process, offering insights into the principles and practices that underpin effective data querying and analysis within the Aitek platform.

Chapter 1.5: Homeland in Aitek: Admin

"Good administration is the keel that keeps the security vessel steadfast."

We delve into the foundational aspect of administration within the platform's configuration hierarchy. Following the initial installation, there exists a single built-in user known as "root," whose default password is set to the serial number of the engine's license. This root user is initially connected to a default repository on PostgreSQL and is endowed with comprehensive default rights, including the capability to create users, roles, groups, families, instances, repositories, datalake spaces (VM+disk), virtual IoT Box spaces and connectors, and spaces for AI containers. Additionally, the root user is equipped to import backups and, within a specific instance, to import a knowledge module. Post-installation, it is strongly recommended to change the root password and to secure the account. This section aims to explore the critical role of the root administrator in the initial configuration and ongoing management of the platform, highlighting the importance of securing the root account to maintain system integrity and security.

the root user can install a license and an update and does not need a license to log in, but has no rights to the application and cannot be assigned any roles other than the default ones.

Root Administration and Initial Configuration: at the core of the platform's administrative structure is the root user, a pivotal entity responsible for the foundational configuration tasks post-installation. This part of the chapter outlines the initial steps undertaken by the root user, including the establishment of the system's primary settings and the configuration of essential components and services.

Comprehensive Default Rights of the Root User: the root user's default rights encompass a broad spectrum of administrative functions critical for setting up and maintaining the platform's operational environment. These rights facilitate the creation and management of user accounts, roles, groups, families, and various data storage and processing spaces. This section details the scope of these rights and their significance in the platform's overall configuration and functionality.

Security Measures for the Root Account: given the root user's extensive access and control over the platform, securing the root account is paramount. Changing the default password and securing the account against unauthorized access are crucial steps in safeguarding the platform's integrity. This part of the chapter discusses best practices for root account security, including password management policies, account locking mechanisms, and the rationale behind these security measures.

Implications for Platform Management and Security: the administration role of the root user has profound implications for the platform's management and security. Effective root administration ensures the proper setup, configuration, and security of the platform, laying the groundwork for its reliable and secure operation. The chapter concludes by reflecting on the importance of root administration in the broader context of platform management, emphasizing the critical nature of securing the root account as a fundamental aspect of the platform's security posture.

The administration of the platform, rooted in the comprehensive default rights and responsibilities of the root user, is essential for the initial configuration, ongoing management, and security of the system. Through meticulous administration and the implementation of robust security measures for the root account, the platform can achieve a high level of operational integrity and resilience. This chapter has provided an in-depth exploration of the role of root administration within the platform's configuration hierarchy, underscoring the importance of securing the root account to maintain the platform's overall security and functionality.

we explore the initial configuration and setup process within the Aitek platform, specifically through the default instance using the root user account. This process includes configuring the engine, installing the license, and, if necessary, creating additional repositories beyond the default (especially if the default Virtual Machine (VM) does not meet requirements) for the datalake. Furthermore, it involves establishing structural roles and designating a user owner for the Knowledge Cartridge, such as HL_Adm (Homeland Admin), and assigning appropriate roles to them. The procedure continues with logging out from the root account, signing in as HL_Adm, and creating the Homeland instance. Subsequently, the setup can proceed in two distinct directions: importing a backup and installing the license for the Knowledge Cartridge, or installing a standard Knowledge Cartridge without customization or sample data/sandbox environments. This section aims to elucidate the steps involved in the initial platform setup, highlighting the critical role of role assignment and Knowledge Cartridge configuration in establishing a functional and secure operational environment.

Engine Configuration and License Installation: the foundational step in setting up the Aitek platform involves configuring the engine using the root user account and installing the platform license. This section details the technical and administrative considerations in engine configuration and license installation, underscoring their importance in activating the platform's functionalities.

Repository Creation and Datalake Configuration: Depending on the platform's data storage and processing needs, additional repositories may need to be created beyond the default setup. This might involve configuring additional VMs for the datalake to accommodate the volume and complexity of the data being managed. This part of the chapter examines the criteria for determining repository and datalake requirements, including storage capacity, access speed, and data security considerations.

Role Assignment and Knowledge Cartridge Ownership: assigning structural roles and designating a Knowledge Cartridge owner, such as HL_Adm for Homeland Admin, are pivotal steps in the platform's configuration. These actions establish the administrative and operational hierarchy within the platform, delineating access rights and responsibilities. The process for role assignment and the implications of designating a module owner are discussed, highlighting the impact on platform governance and operational efficiency.

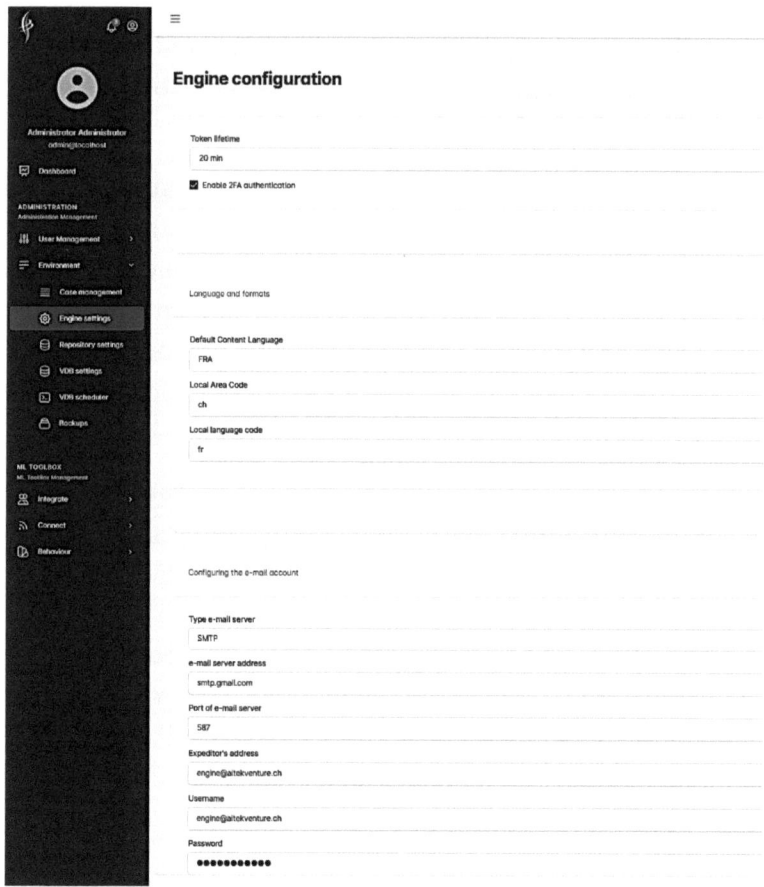

Transitioning from Root to Knowledge Cartridge Administration: the process of logging out from the root account and transitioning to operate under a designated administrator account, such as HL_Adm, signifies a critical shift in platform management. This transition is essential for operational security and the segregation of administrative duties. The chapter explores the procedural and security aspects of this transition, emphasizing best practices for account management and operational integrity.

Knowledge Cartridge Setup: the final step in the initial configuration involves setting up the Knowledge Cartridge, either by importing a backup and installing its license or by installing a standard module. This section delves into the considerations for choosing between these options, including the benefits and limitations of each approach in terms of customization, data handling, and initial operational setup.

The initial configuration and setup of the Aitek platform are crucial for establishing a secure, efficient, and fully functional operational environment. Through careful engine configuration, repository and datalake setup, role assignment, and Knowledge Cartridge installation, the platform is primed for its intended use cases. This chapter has provided a comprehensive guide to the setup process, offering insights into the foundational steps that underpin the platform's operational readiness and security posture.

ADMIN USER

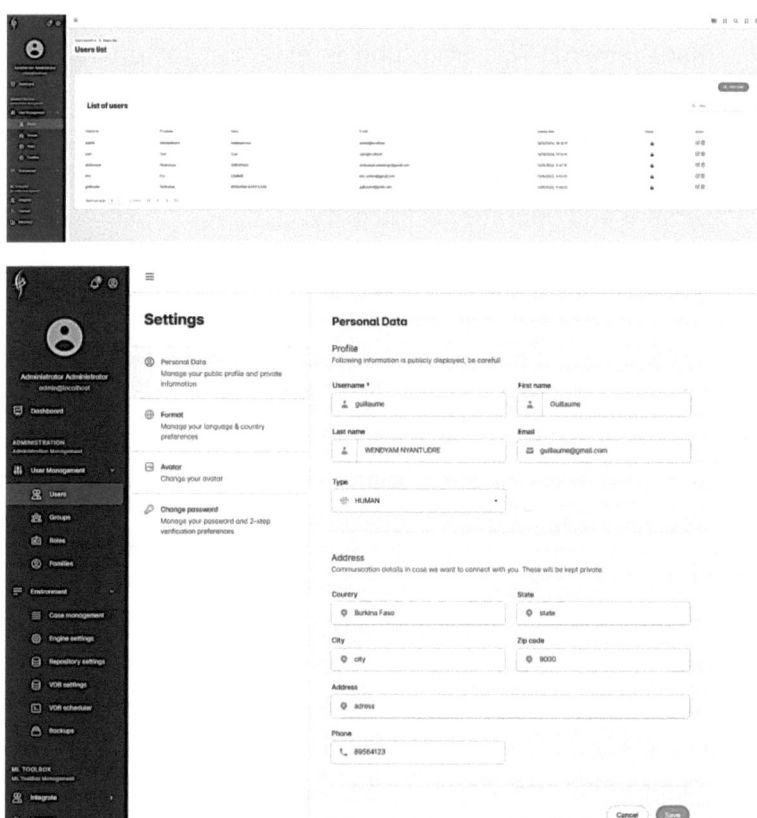

we delve into a crucial aspect of security within the platform, focusing on the enforcement of network mask and MAC address restrictions as a measure to safeguard access. Furthermore, the platform does not rely on external QR code components for mobile devices; instead, it utilizes a mechanism where the mobile device communicates its IMEI and other relevant information. Upon initiating a request, the associated user has a 60-second window to authenticate successfully.

After three unsuccessful attempts, whether due to incorrect password entry or timeout, the user account is locked. In situations involving changes to a user's mobile device or PC, the re-synchronization process is facilitated through a backup email address under the supervision of either a human administrator or an AI-admin agent. This section aims to elucidate the operational framework and strategic implications of these security measures, emphasizing their role in enhancing the platform's integrity and user access control.

Network Mask and MAC Address Restrictions: the implementation of network mask and MAC address restrictions serves as a foundational security measure to control access to the platform. This section explores the technical rationale behind these restrictions, detailing how they contribute to a secure operational environment by limiting access to authorized devices only.

Mobile Device Communication and IMEI Utilization: unlike conventional systems that may use external QR codes for authentication, the platform opts for a direct communication method involving the mobile device's IMEI and pertinent infor-mation. This subsection examines the advantages of this approach, including enhanced security and streamlined user authentication processes.

Authentication Window and Account Locking Mechanisms: the platform employs a 60-second window for user authentication, coupled with a strict policy for account locking after three failed attempts. This part of the chapter discusses the balance between user convenience and security measures, analyzing the impact of these policies on preventing unauthorized access and ensuring user accountability.

Re-synchronization Process for Device or PC Changes: addressing the challenges associated with changing a user's mobile device or PC, the platform facilitates a re-synchronization process through a backup email, under administrative oversight. This section delves into the procedural steps of this process, highlighting the roles of human administrators and AI-admin agents in managing re-synchronization securely and efficiently.

The platform's approach to security, encompassing network mask and MAC address restrictions, direct mobile device communication, stringent authentication policies, and a supervised re-synchronization process, reflects a comprehensive strategy to safeguard access and maintain operational integrity. By providing an in-depth analysis of these security measures and their implementation within the platform, this chapter underscores their significance in the broader context of maintaining a secure, reliable, and user-centric operational framework.

ROLE

In this chapter, we delve into the pivotal role of role-based security mechanisms within the platform architecture, highlighting the distinction between structural roles and nature-based roles. These roles are fundamental to the security and operational integrity of the platform, dictating access rights and permissions through a CRUDE (Create, Read, Update,

Delete, Execute) Matrix across various platform objects such as action plans, roles, devices, objectives, etc. Structural roles primarily govern rights over the platform's objects, while nature-based roles define access to the data within the KnowledgeMart and FlowMart, acting as an implicit "where" clause to filter data access. This system ensures that information outside of a user's query scope is returned in an obfuscated manner, akin to a "burn list." This arrangement ensures that any human or AI agent lacking sufficient privileges but encountering a risk-related piece of information must escalate the issue, thereby guaranteeing that risks are addressed even if the discoverer does not have the necessary clearances to read and act upon the information directly.

Role-Based Security Mechanisms: the foundation of platform security lies in its role-based access control system, which assigns specific permissions and restrictions to various roles. This section explores the design and implementation of these roles, emphasizing the balance between operational flexibility and security.

CRUDE Matrix in Platform Object Management: the CRUDE Matrix serves as a comprehensive framework for defining access rights to platform objects. This matrix is instrumental in detailing the permissions associated with structural roles, facilitating precise control over the creation, reading, updating, deleting, and executing of platform objects. The intricacies of the CRUDE Matrix and its application within the platform are examined, highlighting its role in maintaining data integrity and operational security.

Nature-Based Roles and Data Access: nature-based roles introduce an additional layer of data access control, effectively filtering data visibility based on the role's attributes. This mechanism implements an implicit "where" clause for data queries, ensuring that only relevant and permitted data is accessible to a role. The concept of nature-based roles and their impact on data security and accessibility is discussed, alongside the technical strategies for implementing these access controls.

Data Obfuscation and Risk Escalation: the platform's security architecture incorporates data obfuscation for information outside the permissible query scope, similar to the principles of a burn list. This ensures that sensitive data remains protected, even when accessed by roles without the requisite privileges. The protocol for escalating discovered risks, especially in cases where the discoverer lacks full access rights, is detailed, underlining the system's proactive approach to risk management.

The role-based security framework of the platform, characterized by its structural and nature-based roles alongside the

CRUDE Matrix, provides a robust mechanism for managing access to both platform objects and data. This chapter has outlined the principles and practices underlying this security model, demonstrating its effectiveness in safeguarding sensitive information while ensuring that potential risks are adequately escalated and addressed. Through this meticulous approach to role-based security, the platform ensures a secure, efficient, and responsive operational environment.

the nuanced process of rights assignment within the platform, highlighting the innovative approach where rights can be granted based on roles. This role-based rights assignment mechanism allows for the inheritance of all permissions from an initial role, with the capability to further enrich these permissions as needed. Additionally, this system facilitates the association of one or "n" groups to a specific role, effectively aggregating users within the database under these designated groups. The discussion herein aims to elucidate the mechanisms of role-based rights assignment, the dynamics of rights inheritance and enrichment, and the strategic organization of users into groups for optimized access control and operational efficiency.

Role-Based Rights Assignment: at the core of the platform's security and operational framework is the role-based rights assignment mechanism. This approach not only simplifies the management of permissions but also ensures a granular level of control over access rights across the platform. This section delves into the foundational principles of role-based rights assignment, detailing how roles are defined, associated with specific permissions, and assigned to users or groups within the platform.

Dynamics of Rights Inheritance and Enrichment: a distinctive feature of the platform's rights management system is the ability to inherit permissions from an initial role and subsequently enrich these permissions. This flexibility allows for customized access controls that can be tailored to the specific needs and responsibilities of various user groups. The process of inheriting and enriching rights is examined, with a focus on the mechanisms that enable this dynamic adjustment of permissions.

Organization of Users into Groups: the platform employs a strategic organization of users into groups, based on roles, to streamline access management. This grouping mechanism aggregates users who share common roles, thereby facilitating the efficient assignment of permissions and the management of access rights at a group level. This part of the chapter discusses the criteria for group formation, the benefits of aggregating users into groups, and the impact of this organizational strategy on the platform's overall security posture and operational efficiency.

Implications for Access Control and Operational Efficiency: the role-based rights assignment and the organization of users into groups have significant implications for the platform's access control and operational efficiency. By leveraging roles and groups, the platform can achieve a high level of precision in access management, ensuring that users have the necessary permissions to fulfill their duties without compromising the system's security. The chapter concludes by reflecting on the broader implications of these mechanisms for enhancing the platform's functionality, security, and user experience.

The innovative approach to rights assignment and user organization within the platform represents a sophisticated model for managing access control and enhancing operational efficiency. Through the strategic use of role-based rights assignment, rights inheritance and enrichment, and the aggregation of users into groups, the platform establishes a robust framework for secure and efficient operations. This chapter has provided a comprehensive overview of these mechanisms, offering insights into their importance and implementation within the context of the platform's broader operational and security strategies.

GROUP

we delve into the concept of groups, families, or subgroups within the Aitek platform framework, a crucial mechanism for classifying users—whether human, AI, or simple programs (robots). This classification system is instrumental for operational dynamics, such as linking a task within an action plan to a specific group and subsequently auto-assigning the task to the first available user within that group at the moment of action plan instantiation. Moreover, this grouping mechanism serves as a pivotal business key for navigating the KnowledgeMart during the "check" and "act" phases, which are derived from the associated sub-KnowledgeMarts within Aitek's vector database. The discussion herein aims to elucidate the structuring of groups and their strategic importance in task assignment, operational efficiency, and data management within the platform.

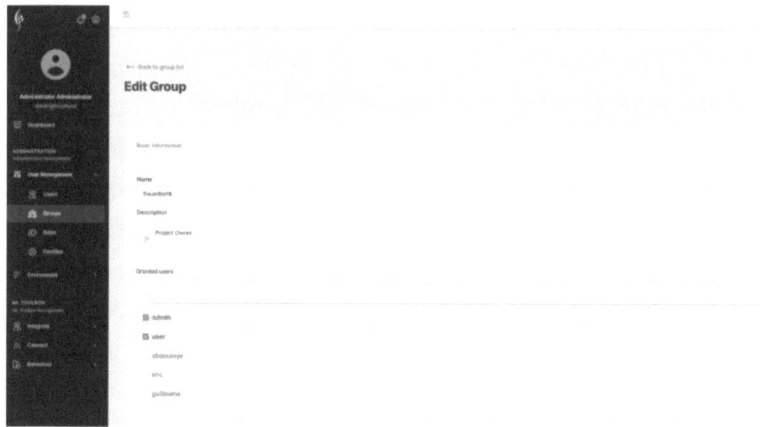

Classification and Group Structuring: the platform's approach to classifying users into groups or families enables a structured and organized management system, accommodating diverse user entities including humans, AI agents, and robots. This section explores the criteria and methodologies employed for user classification, detailing how groups are defined, managed, and utilized within the Aitek ecosystem.

Operational Dynamics of Group Assignment: the assignment of tasks to groups, particularly within action plans, exemplifies the practical application of the group structuring mechanism. By auto-assigning tasks to the first available user in a designated group at the time of action plan instantiation, the platform enhances operational efficiency and ensures timely task execution. This part of the chapter discusses the technical and logistical considerations of this auto-assignment process, including the algorithms and protocols that facilitate dynamic task allocation.

FAMILY

Groups as Business Keys in KnowledgeMart Management: beyond operational efficiency, groups serve as business keys within the platform's KnowledgeMart, especially in the "check" and "act" phases. These phases rely on data from associated sub-KnowledgeMarts within the vector database, where group classification plays a critical role in data navigation and analysis. This section delves into the integration of group structures within the KnowledgeMart framework, examining how they contribute to data segmentation, access control, and analytical insights.

Implications for Data Management and Operational Efficiency: the use of groups, families, or subgroups within the Aitek platform has significant implications for both data management and operational efficiency. By facilitating structured user classification, streamlined task assignment, and nuanced data navigation, groups enhance the platform's functionality and user experience. The chapter concludes by reflecting on the broader impacts of group structuring on the platform's operational dynamics and data management strategies, highlighting the value of this approach in fostering a cohesive and efficient digital ecosystem.

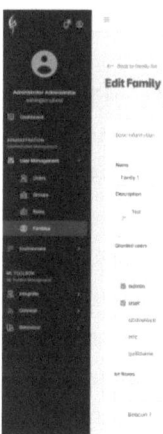

The strategic organization of users into groups, families, or subgroups within the Aitek platform represents a foundational element of the platform's operational and data management framework. Through effective classification and group structuring, the platform achieves a high degree of operational efficiency, precise task assignment, and sophisticated data navigation capabilities. This chapter has provided a comprehensive overview of the role and importance of groups within the Aitek ecosystem, offering insights into their implementation and impact on the platform's overall performance and functionality.

REPOSITORY

We delve into the architecture and functionality of the repository system within the Aitek platform, focusing on its role as a foundational database structure that supports the platform's operation. By default, the repository is based on a SQL database, with PostgreSQL being the standard choice, although it can be adapted to work with Oracle or SQL Server. The repository serves as a crucial storage medium for three distinct types of information: 1) the platform's structural components, including models, setup configurations, and platform objects (roles, action plans, etc.); 2) the organization of non-connectable but applicable data (as outlined in the Datawizzard section), including manual entries; and 3) FlowMart data encompassing performance metrics, reports/simulations, and diagnostics. This exploration aims to elucidate the strategic segmentation of these data types across different repositories for performance and volume considerations, the implications of utilizing multiple repositories on distinct VMs for different data categories, and the recommended practices for repository management within the platform's knowledge instances.

Repository Architecture and Database Types: the repository's foundational role within the Aitek platform is predicated on its ability to support SQL databases, with flexibility in its core database technology. This section examines the considerations behind the choice of PostgreSQL, Oracle, or SQL Server, focusing on the criteria such as performance, scalability, and compatibility with the platform's needs.

Data Segmentation in Repositories: the repository system is designed to accommodate three primary categories of information, each serving distinct operational needs within the platform. This part of the chapter discusses the structural organization of platform components, the management of non-connectable data and its application through manual entries, and the storage and analysis of FlowMart data. The rationale behind segregating these data types into separate repositories is explored, highlighting the benefits for system performance and data manageability.

Performance Optimization through Repository Distribution: for performance optimization and volume management, the platform supports the connection of three different repositories, each housed on separate VMs and dedicated to one of the information categories. This section delves into the technical and operational advantages of distributing data across multiple repositories, considering factors such as load balancing, data retrieval speed, and system resilience.

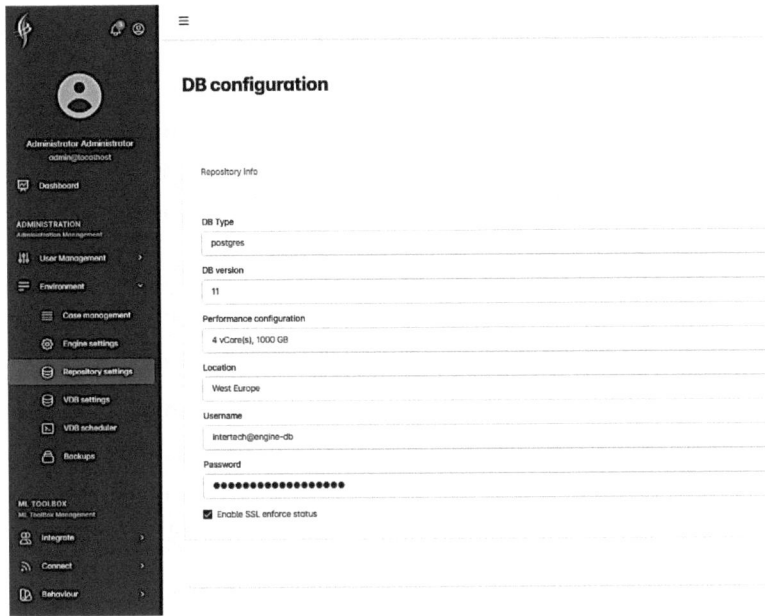

Recommendations for Repository Management: while the platform's architecture permits the splitting of data across multiple repositories, it advises against mixing database types for repositories associated with the same knowledge instance. This part of the chapter outlines the best practices for repository management, emphasizing the importance of consistency in database technology and the strategic allocation of data across repositories.

Configuring Repositories for Knowledge Instances: even though it is technically feasible to store all data within the default repository of the root instance, the chapter advocates for the use of separate repositories for each knowledge instance. This recommendation is predicated on the benefits of tailored data management strategies that enhance the platform's operational efficiency and data integrity.

The repository system within the Aitek platform represents a critical infrastructure component, enabling the structured storage and management of essential data types. Through strategic repository configuration and the judicious segmentation of data, the platform achieves optimal performance and scalability. This chapter has provided a comprehensive overview of the repository system's architecture, its role in the platform's operation, and the best practices for managing repositories to support the diverse needs of knowledge instances, underlining the importance of a well-architected repository system in the broader context of data management and platform functionality.

VDB (VIRTUAL DATABASE) SETUP

In this segment of our exploration, we focus on the structural framework of the vectorial database (VDB) within the Aitek platform, particularly emphasizing the Virtual Machine (VM) that hosts the control APIs, including functions for start, stop, lock, refresh, Query 360, among others. A user of the type VDB (Vectorial Database User) is designated for this database, inheriting the specifics from the user profile. It's crucial to note that locking a VDB user will impede the processes for accessing the database and updating the FlowMart. However, this does not affect the updates to the KnowledgeMart and the computations for anomalies, which will be buffered but will not propagate upwards, effectively placing the database in a de facto locked status. Upon assignment to a knowledge instance, the VDB gains access to the repository information for FlowMart and anomalies, as well as the repository for manual entries, thereby becoming an extension of the datalake. This includes integration with the platform's IoT Box server. This chapter aims to dissect the operational nuances of the VDB within the Aitek ecosystem, examining the implications of user actions on database processes and the integration of various data repositories.

Framework and Control APIs of the VDB: at the heart of the Aitek platform's data processing capabilities is the VM hosting the VDB, equipped with a suite of control APIs for managing the database's operational state. This section outlines the functionalities of these APIs and their pivotal role in maintaining the VDB's integrity and responsiveness.

VDB User Designation and Permissions: Assigning a user with VDB type permissions is a critical step in managing access to the vectorial database. This part of the chapter explores the significance of the VDB user profile, the inheritance of permissions, and the impact of locking a VDB user on the database's operational processes.

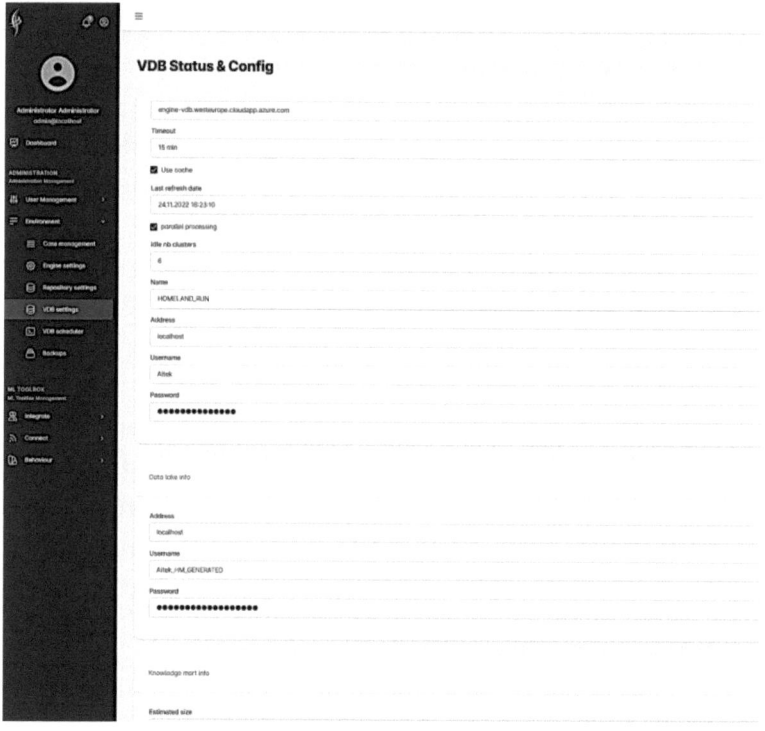

Impact of Locking a VDB User: locking a VDB user has profound implications for the database's accessibility and the flow of data updates, particularly regarding the FlowMart updates versus the unaffected KnowledgeMart updates and anomaly computations. This section delves into the mechanisms of data buffering during lock status and the operational ramifications for the system's alarm functionalities.

Integration with Knowledge Instances and Repositories: the assignment of the VDB to a knowledge instance is a pivotal moment that defines the scope of data access and integration for the VDB. This includes the linking of FlowMart and anomaly data repositories, as well as the incorporation of manual entry repositories into the datalake. This subsection examines the process of repository integration and the extension of the datalake to accommodate diverse data types, including those from the IoT Box server.

The structural and operational framework of the vectorial database within the Aitek platform is fundamental to the system's data management and processing capabilities. Through careful management of VDB user permissions and the strategic integration of data repositories, the platform ensures robust and efficient data handling. This chapter has provided an in-depth analysis of the VDB's role within the Aitek ecosystem, highlighting the critical interactions between database control mechanisms, user management, and data repository integration, underscoring the importance of the VDB in the broader context of the platform's operational efficiency and data integrity.

BACKUP

In this segment of the thesis, we delve into the backup system's framework, focusing on the categorization of backups based on the type of objects they encompass—whether physical or logical—and their location. Additionally, the integration of backup functionality within the instance is examined, particularly how execution frequencies, execution logs, and the capability for restoration are configured and managed. This discussion aims to elucidate the principles underlying the backup strategy within the platform, highlighting the importance of backup operations in ensuring data integrity and system resilience.

Classification of Backup Objects: the foundation of an effective backup system lies in the clear categorization of the objects it aims to protect. This includes distinguishing between physical objects, such as hardware or storage devices, and logical objects, like databases, files, or configurations. This section explores the criteria for classifying objects within the backup framework, examining how the nature of the object influences the backup methodology and technology employed.

Backup Location and Integration: the storage location for backups is a critical aspect of the backup strategy, affecting the ease of access, security, and reliability of the backup data. This part of the chapter discusses the considerations involved in selecting backup locations, including on-site versus off-site storage, cloud-based solutions, and the implications for disaster recovery planning.

Configuring Backup Frequencies and Execution Logs: a key component of the backup system is the ability to configure the frequency of backup operations, tailored to the criticality and dynamic nature of the data being protected. Alongside frequency, the generation and management of execution logs provide transparency and auditability to the backup process. This section delves into the mechanisms for setting backup schedules and maintaining detailed records of backup activities.

Restoration Capabilities: the ultimate test of a backup system's efficacy is its ability to restore data accurately and efficiently following data loss or system failure. The configuration of restoration capabilities within the instance, including the procedures for initiating a restore, the management of restore points, and the validation of restored data, is critically examined. The chapter highlights best practices for ensuring a smooth and reliable restoration process.

The backup system, with its careful categorization of objects, strategic selection of backup locations, configurable execution frequencies, and robust restoration capabilities, forms an essential pillar of data management and system resilience. By dissecting the components and operations of the backup framework, this segment has provided a comprehensive overview of the principles and practices that underpin effective backup strategies within the platform. Emphasizing the integration of backups within the instance and the meticulous management of backup and restoration processes, the discussion underscores the significance of backups in safe-guarding data integrity and ensuring operational continuity.

KNOWLEDGE INSTANCE

We examine the concept and structure of the Knowledge Instance within the Aitek platform, distinguishing it as the physical receptacle for all components of a Knowledge Module. The Knowledge Instance represents the tangible embodiment of the system's data processing capabilities, while the Knowledge Module serves as the logical construct, providing the theoretical framework and tools necessary for users to develop their own customized knowledge modules. This distinction underscores the integration of the vector data-base, repositories, roles, and the loading of Knowledge Mo-dules and associated licenses, including market-available mo-dules like the Homeland and Territorial modules, which are proprietary to Squadbotik SA in Fribourg, Switzerland. Specialized publishers in various industries have contributed to this ecosystem by developing modules complete with test data-sets. In instances where a proprietary module is replicated, the platform's AI oversees copyright integrity, locking new modules that exhibit over 75% similarity to original modules if the original subscription ceases to be paid, as a measure against plagiarism. This section aims to elucidate the operational dynamics of Knowledge Instances and Modules, the legal and ethical considerations in module development and deployment, and the platform's mechanisms for maintaining intellectual property rights.

Knowledge Instance as a Physical Entity: the Knowledge Instance is the foundational element that hosts the vector database, repositories, and roles, enabling the operational deployment of Knowledge Modules. This section details the architecture and functionality of Knowledge Instances, highlighting their role in the physical integration and management of data processing resources within the Aitek platform.

Development and Customization of Knowledge Modules: users are equipped with a comprehensive suite of tools for creating bespoke Knowledge Modules, leveraging the logical framework provided by the platform. This part of the chapter explores the process of module creation, from conceptualization to implementation, emphasizing the user's ability to tailor modules to specific analytical needs and objectives.

Proprietary Knowledge Modules and Licensing: the distinction between proprietary Knowledge Modules developed by Squadbotik SA and those available in the market introduces a layer of intellectual property considerations. The Homeland and Territorial modules serve as examples of proprietary content, necessitating licensing agreements for their use. This section examines the licensing framework wi-thin the Aitek platform, focusing on the legal and operational implications of utilizing proprietary modules.

AI Oversight and Plagiarism Control: a notable feature of the Aitek platform is its AI-driven mechanism for monitoring the similarity between Knowledge Modules. This system ensures the protection of intellectual property by identifying and locking new modules that significantly replicate the content of existing, proprietary modules without proper licensing. The criteria for determining similarity and the process of module locking are discussed, alongside the implications for developers and users within the platform ecosystem.

The Knowledge Instance and Module framework within the Aitek platform represents a sophisticated approach to data analysis and intellectual property management. By delineating between the physical and logical components of knowledge processing and introducing mechanisms for customization, licensing, and plagiarism control, the platform fosters an environment of innovation while safeguarding the rights of content creators. This chapter has provided a comprehensive overview of the Knowledge Instance and Module system, highlighting its significance in the broader context of data processing, module development, and intellectual property rights within the Aitek ecosystem.

Chapter 1.6: Homeland in Aitek: Supervisor

"Vigilant oversight is the beacon that guides safety through the stormy seas of uncertainty."

In this chapter, we explore the Supervisor as a pivotal user interface within the Aitek platform for accessing the Knowledge Module. This interface has evolved from being solely web-based up to version Aitek 6.3, to also include mobile accessibility starting with version 6.4. The introduction of mobile access was not delayed due to the complexity of the interface design but rather due to the intricate requirements of ensuring robust security measures. Through the Supervisor interface, users manage the oversight and processing of alarms and action plans, including their scheduling, supervise organizational performance and risk, initiate queries to the KnowledgeMart (Query 360), and utilize predictive dashboards and reporting tools. Additionally, it offers simulation capabilities and "war gaming" to test the validity of hypotheses. This section aims to elucidate the functionalities provided by the Supervisor interface, emphasizing its role in facilitating comprehensive operational management and strategic decision-making within the platform.

Evolution of the Supervisor Interface: the transition of the Su-pervisor interface from web-only access to include mobile platforms marks a significant evolution in user interaction with the Aitek platform. This part of the chapter details the development timeline and the strategic decisions behind expanding access modalities, with a focus on the challenges and solutions related to implementing mobile access, particularly in the realm of security.

Management of Alarms and Action Plans: central to the Supervisor's functionality is the management of alarms and the scheduling and execution of action plans. This section discusses the interface's capabilities in organizing and responding to operational alerts, coordinating response strategies, and ensuring timely execution of planned actions.

Supervision of Performance and Risk: the Supervisor interface serves as a critical tool for monitoring organizational performance and identifying potential risks. This subsection explores how the interface facilitates real-time oversight of key performance indicators and risk factors, enabling proactive management and mitigation strategies.

KnowledgeMart Queries and Predictive Dashboards: query 360 and predictive dashboards represent essential features of the Supervisor interface, providing powerful tools for data interrogation and insight generation. The chapter examines the functionalities of these features, including their application in predictive analytics, reporting, and the support they offer for strategic planning and operational optimization.

Simulation and War Gaming: the Supervisor interface's simulation and "war gaming" capabilities offer users a unique opportunity to test hypotheses and validate strategic decisions in a controlled environment. This part of the chapter delves into the mechanics and applications of these features, highlighting their value in enhancing decision-making confidence and organizational resilience.

The Supervisor interface is a cornerstone of the Aitek platform, enabling users to seamlessly interact with the Knowledge Module and manage a wide array of operational and strategic functions. By providing comprehensive access to alarms, action plans, performance metrics, and advanced analytical tools, the Supervisor facilitates effective organizational management and decision-making. This chapter has provided an in-depth analysis of the Supervisor's features and functionalities, underscoring its significance in the broader context of the platform's operational ecosystem and strategic capabilities.

HOME

we examine the "Home" interface of the application, which serves as the initial point of entry for users into the system. The Home interface is designed to provide a comprehensive overview of the most recent alarms and action plans relevant to the logged-in user, alongside a map that displays the default Aitek Zone attributed to the user and the geographical positioning of alarms and clusters within their designated area. This section aims to elucidate the functionalities and design principles of the Home interface, highlighting its role in facilitating user engagement with the system, providing situational awareness, and enabling efficient navigation through the application's features.

Overview and Functionality of the Home Interface: the Home interface acts as the central dashboard for users upon entering the application, designed to immediately present critical information that demands the user's attention. This part of the chapter details the layout and components of the Home interface, including how recent alarms and action plans are displayed and updated in real-time to reflect the current operational status.

Integration of Geographical Information: a key feature of the Home interface is the integration of a map that visualizes the Aitek Zone designated to the user, along with the positioning of alarms and clusters within this zone. This section explores the implementation of geographical information systems (GIS) within the interface, discussing the technology's role in enhancing the user's situational awareness and aiding in the strategic planning of responses to alarms and security events.

User-Centric Design and Customization: the Home interface is tailored to present information relevant to the specific user, ensuring that each user's experience is personalized and directly applicable to their role and responsibilities within the system. This subsection examines the design principles that underpin this user-centric approach, including the customization options available to users for modifying the interface to suit their preferences and operational needs.

Navigational Efficiency and User Engagement: The strategic layout and functionality of the Home interface are critical for ensuring efficient navigation through the application's various features and enhancing user engagement with the system. This part of the chapter discusses how the interface design facilitates quick access to essential functions and information, supporting users in making informed decisions and effectively managing security events.

The Home interface represents a critical component of the application, serving as the primary gateway for users into the system and providing a centralized overview of pertinent information and operational statuses. By offering a personalized and geographically informed view of alarms, action plans, and clusters, the "Home" interface enhances users' situational awareness and operational efficiency. This chapter has provided an in-depth analysis of the Home interface's design, functionality, and role in the broader context of the application, emphasizing its importance in supporting user engagement and effective system navigation.

MAP

We delve into the functionality and significance of the map feature within the platform, which serves as a physical representation of one or multiple zones, including the events occurring within these areas. The map is dynamically updated following each refresh of the KnowledgeMart, ensuring that the latest data is always displayed. A critical feature of this map interface is the "real-time" button, which triggers updates of information at a frequency corresponding to real-time indices, as detailed in the chapter on the vector database. This section aims to elucidate the operational mechanics of the map feature, its integration with the platform's data systems, and the implications for user interaction and data analysis.

Map Feature and Zone Representation: the map provides users with a visual representation of geographical zones and the events occurring within these zones. This part of the chapter describes the design and functionality of the map interface, including how zones are delineated and how events are represented and updated on the map.

Integration with the KnowledgeMart: the dynamic nature of the map, with updates following each refresh of the KnowledgeMart, highlights the tight integration between the map feature and the platform's underlying data systems. This section explores the process by which data from the KnowledgeMart is translated into visual updates on the map, including the technical mechanisms that facilitate this integration.

Real-Time Updates and Frequency of Indices: the "real-time" button on the map interface enables users to receive updates at a frequency that mirrors the real-time indices stored within the vector database. This subsection delves into the significance of real-time data refreshment for operational awareness and decision-making, examining how this functionality enhances the map's utility as a tool for monitoring and responding to events.

User Interaction and Data Analysis Implications: the map feature's ability to provide a geographical context for data analysis has profound implications for user interaction with the platform. This part of the chapter discusses how the map facilitates a more intuitive understanding of events and trends within specific zones, supporting users in making informed decisions based on spatial data analysis.

The map feature within the platform stands as a powerful tool for visualizing and interacting with geographical data, enhancing the platform's capability to represent and analyze events within designated zones. By offering real-time updates and integrating closely with the KnowledgeMart and vector database, the map feature significantly contributes to the platform's overall functionality and user experience. This chapter has provided a comprehensive overview of the map's design, functionality, and its role in the broader context of the platform's data analysis and operational management capabilities.

ALARM ON CLUSTER

we explore the geographical representation of sub-clusters on the map interface within the platform, where each sub-cluster is depicted as a circle. The center of this circle is determined by the centroid of the coordinates of the present members, with a stipulation that the radius should not exceed 500 meters; otherwise, an additional circle is to be formed. The name of the cluster is inscribed on the circle, which is color-coded to indicate the current status: green signifies that there is nothing to report, red indicates an unacknowledged alarm, and yellow denotes an ongoing action plan. Furthermore, the intensity of the color corresponds to the level of hostility associated with the cluster. This section aims to elucidate the mechanisms behind the visual representation of sub-clusters, the significance of the color-coding system, and the implications of color intensity for understanding the security dynamics within a given geographical area.

Geographical Representation of Sub-Clusters: the map's design principles for illustrating sub-clusters as circles with a defined radius provide a clear and intuitive visual method for representing the spatial distribution and extent of these groups. This part of the chapter delves into the rationale behind using circles for sub-cluster representation, including the mathematical determination of centroids and the operational reasoning for the 500-meter radius limit.

Color-Coding System for Cluster Status: the color-coding system—green, red, and yellow—serves as an immediate visual indicator of the status of each sub-cluster. This section explores the design and implementation of this system, detailing how it enables users to quickly assess the current state of affairs within each sub-cluster at a glance.

Intensity of Color and Cluster Hostility: the innovative use of color intensity to indicate the level of hostility associated with a cluster introduces an additional layer of information into the map's visual language. This subsection examines the methodology for quantifying and representing hostility levels through color intensity, discussing the implications for situational awareness and decision-making.

Implications for Security Analysis and Operational Decision-Making: the map's ability to convey complex geographical and operational information through simple visual cues significantly enhances the platform's utility for security analysis and operational planning. This part of the chapter discusses the broader implications of the sub-cluster representation system for enhancing user understanding of security situations and supporting informed, strategic decision-making processes.

The visualization of sub-clusters on the map interface, characterized by its clear geographical representation, color-coding for status indication, and color intensity for hostility levels, stands as a vital feature of the platform. By providing users with an intuitive and information-rich visual tool, the platform facilitates enhanced situational awareness, security analysis, and strategic operational planning. This chapter has provided a comprehensive overview of the design, functionality, and operational significance of the sub-cluster representation system, emphasizing its importance in the broader context of the platform's data visualization and analysis capabilities

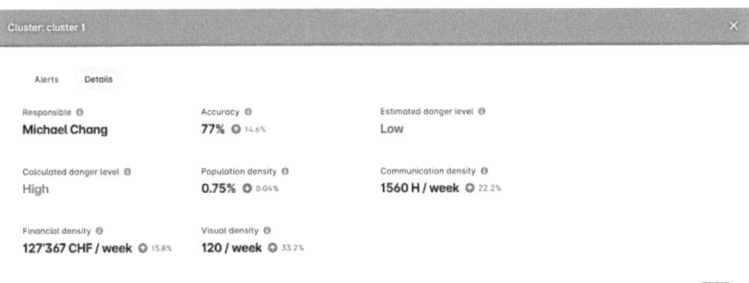

In the event of clicking on a sub-cluster within the platform, users are presented with an alarm panel similar to that found on the "Home" page, albeit filtered specifically for the selected sub-cluster of the zone. This tailored interface provides

access not only to the information pertaining to the members currently present within this sub-cluster but also to comprehensive data encompassing the entire cluster. Additionally, this panel facilitates direct communication with the cluster's supervisor, allowing users to contact or leave a message for the supervisor directly from this interface. This chapter aims to dissect the functionality and user experience of interacting with sub-clusters through the platform, emphasizing the significance of the filtered alarm panel, the accessibility of member and cluster-wide information, and the communication features that enhance coordination and response strategies within the platform's operational framework.

Functionality of the Sub-Cluster Click Response: upon selecting a sub-cluster, the platform's response mechanism activates a context-specific alarm panel. This section explores the technical and design considerations behind this feature, detailing how the alarm panel is filtered to present data relevant to the selected sub-cluster and enhancing the user's navigational experience within the platform.

Access to Member and Cluster-Wide Information: The filtered panel extends beyond displaying alarms, offering users comprehensive access to information about members within the sub-cluster as well as overarching cluster data. This part of the chapter delves into the mechanisms for aggregating and presenting this information, examining the platform's capability to provide a holistic view of the cluster's operational status and member activities.

Direct Communication with the Cluster Supervisor: a key feature of the sub-cluster interface is the ability to facilitate direct communication with the cluster supervisor. This section discusses the importance of this communication channel in fostering effective coordination and oversight within clusters. It explores the interface's design for message exchange and the potential impact on operational efficiency and response coordination.

Implications for Operational Coordination and Response: the integration of a context-specific alarm panel, combined with access to detailed member information and direct communication capabilities, significantly impacts the platform's operational coordination and response strategies. This part of the chapter reflects on the broader implications of these features for enhancing situational awareness, streamlining decision-making processes, and improving the overall effectiveness of operational responses within the platform's ecosystem.

The functionality provided by the platform upon interacting with a sub-cluster – ranging from the display of a contextually filtered alarm panel to the facilitation of direct communication with cluster supervisors – represents a sophisticated approach to managing operational data and enhancing user engagement. By offering tailored access to critical information and communication tools, the platform supports a more informed and coordinated approach to security and operational management. This chapter has provided an in-depth analysis of the user experience and operational benefits associated with sub-cluster interaction, underscoring its importance in the broader context of the platform's data visualization and analysis capabilities.

FOLLOW UP

We delve into the follow-up mechanisms implemented within the Aitek platform for tracking cluster statistics. This analysis draws upon data from FlowMart indicators and detected anomalies, utilizing standard temporal aggregations—day, week, month, quarter, semester, and year—to provide a comprehensive overview of cluster performance over time. Additionally, this system incorporates group by functionalities, which include business entities from the Aitek Knowledge Model, enhancing the granularity and specificity of the data analysis. From within the detailed view, users have the capability to initiate a Cluster 360 analysis, with date parameters automatically set to reflect the current cluster's timeframe and granularity selected – such as monthly from the first to the last day of the month – covering all information pertinent to the cluster. This chapter aims to elucidate the structure and function of the follow-up system within the Aitek platform, emphasizing its role in facilitating in-depth statistical analysis and operational insights for clusters.

Temporal Aggregations and Data Analysis: the backbone of the follow-up system is its use of temporal aggregations to organize and interpret cluster data over specified time periods. This section explores the methodology behind these aggregations and their application in analyzing cluster performance and trends over time, providing a nuanced understanding of cluster dynamics.

Integration of Business Entities in Data Analysis: beyond temporal aggregations, the follow-up system employs group by functionalities that leverage business entities from the

Aitek Knowledge Model. This part of the chapter discusses the significance of incorporating these entities into data analysis, detailing how this approach enhances the depth and relevance of the insights generated.

Cluster 360 Analysis: a pivotal feature of the follow-up system is the ability to launch a Cluster 360 analysis directly from the detailed view of cluster statistics. This subsection examines the operational mechanics and analytical advantages of the Cluster 360 analysis, including how date parameters and granularity choices impact the scope and focus of the analysis.

Operational Insights and Decision Support: the comprehensive data analysis facilitated by the follow-up system, including temporal aggregations, business entity integration, and Cluster 360 analysis, provides a rich foundation for operational insights and decision-making. This section reflects on the implications of these analytical capabilities for strategic planning, operational optimization, and risk management within the platform's ecosystem.

The follow-up system within the Aitek platform represents a sophisticated analytical toolset for monitoring and evaluating cluster statistics, employing temporal aggregations, business entity integration, and advanced Cluster 360 analysis to generate deep insights into cluster performance and anomalies. By offering a structured approach to data analysis and insight generation, the follow-up system significantly enhances the platform's ability to support informed decision-making and strategic operational management. This chapter has provided a comprehensive overview of the follow-up system's functionalities and its importance in the broader context of data-driven operational oversight within the Aitek platform.

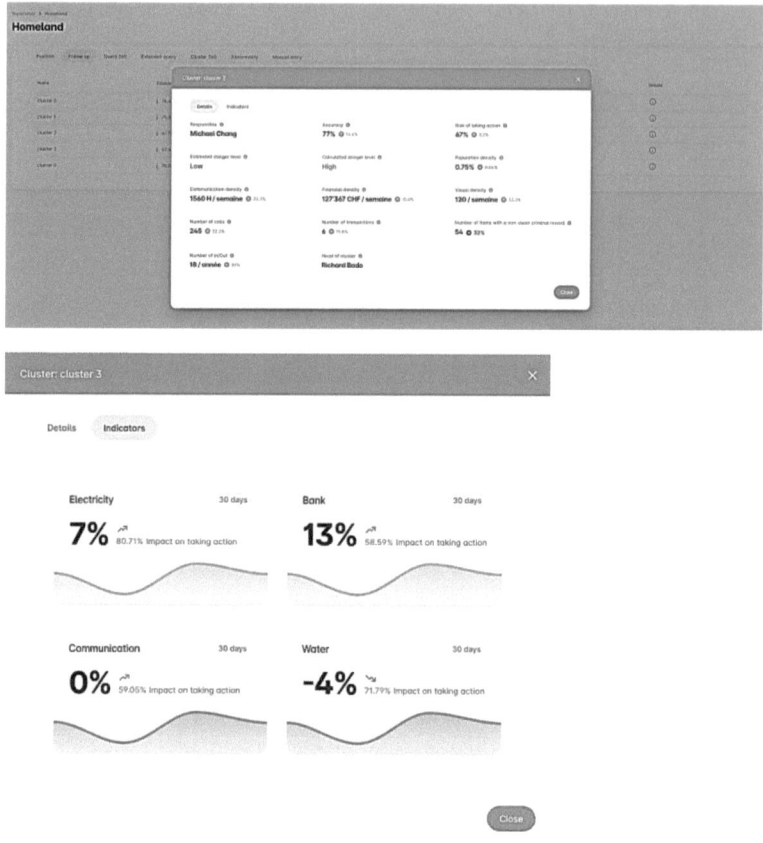

CLUSTER 360

This interface generates a query that executes on the Aitek vector database engine through APIs, conducting an interrogation of the KnowledgeMart with a "where" clause focused on the cluster ID. This operation exemplifies the sophisticated interaction between user interfaces and the underlying data management systems within the platform. By leveraging the vector database engine and its associated APIs, the platform enables precise and targeted queries that sift through the extensive KnowledgeMart based on specific criteria, such as cluster identification. This section of the thesis aims to dissect the technical mechanisms and operational implications of this query generation process, highlighting its significance in facilitating data retrieval and analysis within the Aitek platform's ecosystem.

The Cluster 360 feature within the platform represents a pivotal tool for delineating the composition of a cluster based on member classification: active members, Fit members, and Sympathizers. This functionality enables the execution of a Query 360 specifically targeted at an individual user within the cluster. This section of the thesis delves into the operational framework and analytical capabilities of the Cluster 360 feature, highlighting its role in refining the understanding of cluster dynamics by categorizing members according to their engagement level and potential influence within the cluster. Additionally, the capacity to initiate a Query 360 on a singular user offers a nuanced approach to data analysis, allowing for a detailed examination of individual contributions and behaviors within the broader cluster context.

Classification of Cluster Members: the Cluster 360 feature's ability to classify members into distinct categories—Active, Fit, and Sympathizer—provides a structured mechanism for assessing the engagement and influence levels of individuals within a cluster. This part of the chapter explores the criteria used to categorize members, the significance of each category in understanding cluster dynamics, and the implications for cluster management and strategic planning.

Operational Mechanics of Cluster 360: the operational mechanics behind the Cluster 360 feature, including the algorithms and data models that support member classification and the execution of targeted queries, are examined in this section. The discussion focuses on the technological underpinnings that enable the feature's analytical capabilities, providing insight into the sophisticated data processing and analysis framework that supports Cluster 360 operations.

Query 360 Targeting Individual Users: a critical functionality within the Cluster 360 feature is the ability to launch a Query 360 aimed at an individual user, offering a granular perspective on user-specific data and behaviors. This sub-section delves into the process of initiating such queries, the types of information that can be extracted, and the potential applications of this data in enhancing the understanding of individual roles and impacts within the cluster.

Implications for Cluster Analysis and Management: the comprehensive analysis capabilities afforded by the Cluster 360 feature have significant implications for cluster analysis and management. By enabling detailed examination of cluster composition and individual member analysis, the feature supports nuanced decision-making and strategic interventions. This section reflects on the broader implications of the Cluster 360 feature for organizational strategy, operational efficiency, and the cultivation of insights into cluster dynamics.

The Cluster 360 feature stands as a testament to the platform's advanced analytical capabilities, offering a sophisticated tool for dissecting cluster composition and individual member behaviors. Through the classification of members and the provision of targeted query functionalities, Cluster 360 enhances the platform's ability to support detailed analysis and informed decision-making. This chapter has provided an in-depth exploration of the Cluster 360 feature's operational framework, its role in facilitating comprehensive cluster analysis, and its importance in the broader context of data-driven cluster management within the platform.

QUERY 360

In this section, we delve into the intricacies of an interface designed to generate queries that operate at the most granular level of aggregation within the vector database engine, facilitated through API integration. This interface conducts a detailed interrogation of the KnowledgeMart, utilizing a "where" clause that specifies the information of analytical entities as configured in the engine, alongside a defined date range. This query is designed to retrieve a comprehensive set of fields, making them "visible on the screen" according to the core system's configuration. Notably, the batch mode feature of this query process enables the extraction of the entire KnowledgeMart table into an encrypted CSV file. The encryption key for this file is the public user ID of the individual who initiated the file request. This chapter aims to explore the operational framework of this query generation process, emphasizing its role in enabling deep data analysis and extraction within the platform's ecosystem.

Query Generation and Execution Mechanics: the foundational aspect of this functionality is the generation and execution of queries that penetrate to the lowest level of data aggregation within the vector database engine. This subsection examines the technical architecture supporting this process, focusing on the utilization of APIs to facilitate direct interaction with the database engine and the formulation of queries that precisely target specific analytical entities and date ranges.

Interrogation of the KnowledgeMart with Specific Parameters: central to the platform's analytical prowess is the KnowledgeMart, a comprehensive repository of the platform's accumulated knowledge and data. The capability to interrogate the KnowledgeMart with finely tuned parameters, including analytical entity information and date ranges, highlights the system's sophisticated data retrieval mecha-nisms. This section delves into how these interrogations are structured and the impact of such targeted queries on the visibility and accessibility of data fields within the user interface.

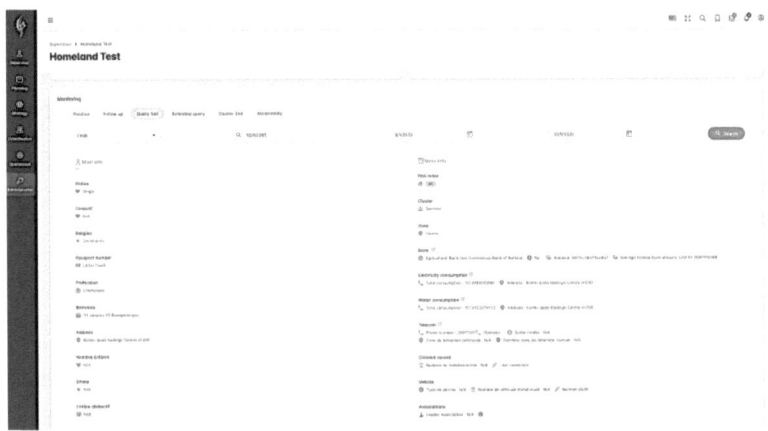

Batch Mode for Comprehensive Data Extraction: a notable feature of this query process is the batch mode, which allows for the extraction of the entire KnowledgeMart database into an encrypted CSV file. This subsection explores the technical and operational considerations of this feature, including the encryption process and the use of the requester's user ID as the encryption key. The implications of this feature for data security, user privacy, and the efficient handling of large data volumes are discussed in detail.

The interface's ability to generate and execute highly granular queries within the vector database engine, coupled with its capacity for detailed interrogation of the KnowledgeMart, represents a significant advancement in the platform's data analysis and extraction capabilities. By providing users with the tools to retrieve detailed datasets based on specific parameters and to export comprehensive data tables securely, the platform enhances its utility for in-depth data analysis and operational insight generation. This chapter has provided a comprehensive overview of the query generation process, its integration with the platform's data management system, and the operational benefits of the batch mode data extraction feature, underscoring its importance in the broader context of the platform's analytical functionalities.

MANUEL ENTRY

In this section, we explore the functionality and implications of measures (the terminal nodes of the model) that are applicable but not directly connectable within the datalake. The application addresses this by generating an order entry and implementing a system for storing results in a repository specifically linked to the knowledge instance. This segment of the repository, in effect, becomes an extension of the data-lake associated with the knowledge instance. This chapter aims to dissect the mechanisms behind the generation of order entries for non-connectable measures, the storage of results in a dedicated repository, and the integration of this repository as an extension of the datalake, emphasizing its significance in enhancing the platform's data analysis and management capabilities.

Handling of Non-Connectable Measures in the Datalake: the initial focus is on the treatment of measures within the model that, due to their nature, cannot be directly connected to the existing datalake structure. This section delves into the operational framework that identifies these measures and outlines the process for generating order entries, facilitating their application within the system's analytical workflows.

Result Storage in a Specific Repository: upon generating order entries for these non-connectable measures, the platform channels the resulting data into a repository that is uniquely associated with the relevant knowledge instance. This subsection examines the structure and function of this specialized repository, including its configuration, management, and the role it plays in preserving the integrity and accessibility of the resultant data.

Integration as an Extension of the Datalake: the transformation of a segment of the repository into an extension of the datalake associated with a particular knowledge instance represents a critical innovation in the platform's data management strategy. This part of the chapter explores the implications of this integration for data analysis, the seamless extension of the datalake's capabilities, and the enhancement of the knowledge instance's operational effectiveness.

Implications for Data Analysis and Knowledge Management: the capability to extend the datalake through the inclusion of results from non-connectable measures significantly broadens the analytical horizon of the knowledge instance. This section reflects on the broader implications of this functionality for the platform's data analysis and knowledge management capabilities, emphasizing how it supports a more comprehensive and nuanced understanding of the data landscape.

The methodology for managing non-connectable measures within the platform, particularly the generation of order entries and the strategic storage of results in a repository linked to the knowledge instance, exemplifies a sophisticated approach to data analysis and management. By effectively extending the datalake to include these measures, the platform enhances its analytical depth and operational efficiency. This chapter has provided an in-depth analysis of the processes and implications of integrating non-connectable measures into the platform's data ecosystem, underscoring its importance in the broader context of the platform's capabilities for data management and analysis.

EXTENDED QUERY

In the context of advanced data management and query optimization within the Aitek platform, starting from version 6.5, an enhanced query functionality becomes activated when the replication option on the vector database is enabled. This feature, referred to as the "extended query," enables a comprehensive 360-degree analysis across the shared database infrastructure.

The implementation of this extended query mechanism signifies a pivotal advancement in how data is accessed, analyzed, and leveraged within the platform. By facilitating a 360-degree view, it allows users to conduct thorough examinations of data from multiple perspectives, enhancing the depth and breadth of insights that can be extracted. This holistic approach to data querying is particularly beneficial in environments where the complexity and volume of data necessitate sophisticated analysis techniques to derive meaningful information.

The activation of replication on the vector database serves as a catalyst for this enhanced querying capability. Vector databases, known for their efficiency in handling complex queries and large datasets, become even more powerful with replication enabled. Replication not only improves data availability and fault tolerance but also significantly enhances performance for read-intensive operations. In this scenario, the extended query leverages the replicated data to provide a more efficient, comprehensive, and robust querying experience.

This extended querying functionality, introduced in version 6.5 of the Aitek platform, underscores the platform's commitment to continuous improvement and innovation in data management. It represents a strategic response to the evolving needs of users who require advanced tools for data analysis in order to make informed decisions in a timely manner. By offering a 360-degree view on a replicated vector database, the platform ensures that users have access to a highly efficient, reliable, and comprehensive data analysis tool.

The significance of this development extends beyond the technical realm, highlighting the importance of adaptive and scalable data management strategies in today's data-driven landscape. As organizations continue to grapple with the challenges posed by big data, innovations such as the extended query feature of the Aitek platform provide a blue-print for how platforms can evolve to meet these challenges head-on, thereby enabling users to unlock the full potential of their data assets.

ANORMALITY

In the intricate architecture of modern data ecosystems, anomalies represent critical signals that necessitate rigorous analysis and contextual interpretation. Within the framework of the knowledge model, each anomaly is intricately linked to a specific node, reflecting a contextual relationship that is essential for comprehensive understanding and effective management of these irregularities. This connection serves as the foundation for a sophisticated alarm mechanism, which acts as an initial point of detection and response to these anomalies.

The subsequent flow of information from these detected anomalies into the data lake forms a crucial component of the data management strategy, facilitating the creation of sub KnowledgeMarts. These specialized repositories are designed to support targeted analysis and deeper insights into specific categories of anomalies, thereby enhancing the granularity and relevance of the data analysis process. This mechanism, referred to as "Anomaly 360," empowers stakeholders to conduct focused queries on targeted anomalies, enabling a more nuanced and effective approach to anomaly management.

The Anomaly 360 concept underscores the importance of a holistic approach to anomaly detection and analysis. By integrating anomalies into the broader knowledge model and ensuring their information flows into dedicated analytical repositories, organizations can achieve a 360-degree view of these phenomena. This comprehensive perspective is essential for identifying underlying patterns, assessing potential impacts, and formulating appropriate responses to mitigate risks associated with these anomalies.

Moreover, the integration of anomaly data into sub KnowledgeMarts facilitates a more dynamic and adaptive data analytics framework. It enables organizations to refine their analytical models continuously, enhance their predictive capabilities, and develop more robust strategies for managing the complexities of the data landscape. This approach not only improves the accuracy and efficiency of anomaly detection and analysis but also contributes to the overall resilience and intelligence of the data ecosystem.

In summary, the Anomaly 360 framework represents a sophisticated approach to managing and analyzing anomalies within the context of a knowledge model. By ensuring a seamless flow of anomaly-related information into dedicated data repositories and enabling targeted analysis, this frame-work provides a comprehensive and effective mechanism for understanding and addressing anomalies. This approach not only enhances the quality of insights derived from anomaly analysis but also significantly contributes to the strategic management of data and information within organizations, ultimately supporting more informed decision-making and risk management practices.

ALARM

In this section, we examine the functionality of an interface within the platform that is pivotal for managing alarm information. This interface grants users the capability to view alarm details with the intention to either dismiss the alarm, validate it, or initiate the associated action plan. Crucially, it also offers the option to instruct the artificial intelligence (AI) system to "do the same" for future occurrences that are similar in nature. This chapter aims to dissect the operational mechanics and strategic implications of this interface, highlighting its role in streamlining the alarm management process and enhancing the platform's responsiveness through AI integration.

Alarm Management Interface Capabilities: the core functionality of this interface lies in its ability to provide a comprehensive overview of an alarm's information, enabling users to make informed decisions regarding its handling. This section delves into the design and functionality of the inter-face, emphasizing how it facilitates user interaction with alarm data and supports critical decision-making processes.

User Actions and Alarm Resolution: central to the interface's utility is the range of actions it affords the user, including the ability to ignore, validate, or act upon an alarm. This subsection explores the procedural and operational aspects of these actions, detailing the mechanisms by which users can resolve alarms and the impact of these resolutions on the overall system efficacy.

AI Integration for Future Occurrence Management: a distinctive feature of the interface is its capability to communicate user decisions to the platform's AI, specifically the instruction to "do the same" for similar future occurrences. This part of the chapter examines the technical integration of AI decision-making within the alarm management process, analyzing how this feature enhances the platform's adaptability and efficiency in handling recurring alarm scenarios.

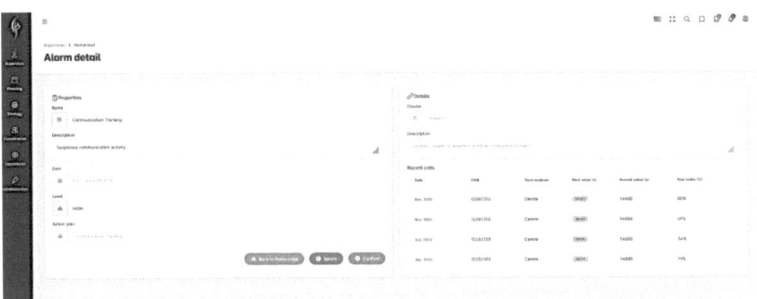

Implications for Operational Efficiency and AI Responsiveness: the integration of user-guided AI decision-making in the alarm management interface has significant implications for the platform's operational efficiency and the responsiveness of its AI systems. This section reflects on the broader impact of this functionality, considering how it contributes to a more dynamic and intelligent system capable of learning from user inputs and automating responses to common alarm scenarios.

The alarm management interface, with its comprehensive functionality and AI integration, represents a crucial component of the platform, enabling effective alarm resolution and leveraging AI to automate responses to recurring scenarios. By providing users with the tools to interact with, assess, and direct the handling of alarms, the interface significantly contributes to the platform's operational efficiency and intelligence. This chapter has provided an in-depth exploration of the interface's capabilities and its importance in the broader context of the platform's alarm management and AI responsiveness strategies.

ACTION PLAN

In this section, we examine the functionality of an interface within the platform that is pivotal for managing alarm information. This interface grants users the capability to view alarm details with the intention to either dismiss the alarm, validate it, or initiate the associated action plan. Crucially, it also offers the option to instruct the artificial intelligence (AI) system to "do the same" for future occurrences that are similar in nature. This chapter aims to dissect the operational mechanics and strategic implications of this interface, highlighting its role in streamlining the alarm management process and enhancing the platform's responsiveness through AI integration.

Alarm Management Interface Capabilities: the core functionality of this interface lies in its ability to provide a comprehensive overview of an alarm's information, enabling users to make informed decisions regarding its handling. This section delves into the design and functionality of the interface, emphasizing how it facilitates user interaction with alarm data and supports critical decision-making processes.

User Actions and Alarm Resolution: Central to the interface's utility is the range of actions it affords the user, including the ability to ignore, validate, or act upon an alarm. This subsection explores the procedural and operational aspects of these actions, detailing the mechanisms by which users can resolve alarms and the impact of these resolutions on the overall system efficacy.

AI Integration for Future Occurrence Management: a distinctive feature of the interface is its capability to communicate user decisions to the platform's AI, specifically the instruction to "do the same" for similar future occurrences. This part of the chapter examines the technical integration of AI decision-making within the alarm management process, analyzing how this feature enhances the platform's adaptability and efficiency in handling recurring alarm scenarios.

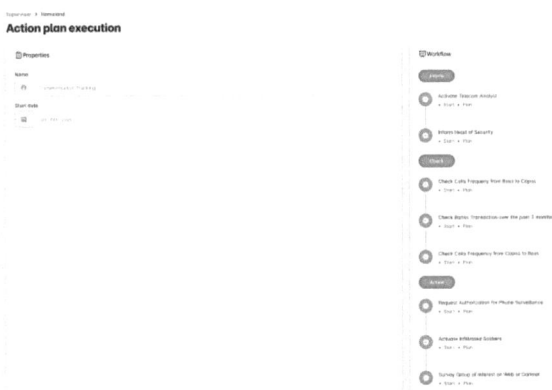

Implications for Operational Efficiency and AI Responsiveness: the integration of user-guided AI decision-making in the alarm management interface has significant implications for the platform's operational efficiency and the responsiveness of its AI systems. This section reflects on the broader impact of this functionality, considering how it contributes to a more dynamic and intelligent system capable of learning from user inputs and automating responses to common alarm scenarios.

The alarm management interface, with its comprehensive functionality and AI integration, represents a crucial component of the platform, enabling effective alarm resolution and leveraging AI to automate responses to recurring scenarios. By providing users with the tools to interact with, assess, and direct the handling of alarms, the interface significantly contributes to the platform's operational efficiency and intelligence. This chapter has provided an in-depth exploration of the interface's capabilities and its importance in the broader context of the platform's alarm management and AI responsiveness strategies.

we underscore the critical process whereby alarm information and action plan data are reintegrated into the data lake through Aitek's Datawizzard tool. This reintegration serves as the primary source material for the sub-KnowledgeMart segments "CHECK" and "ACT," respectively. The chapter aims to dissect the operational mechanisms and strategic significance of funneling this specific data back into the data lake, emphasizing its role in enriching the platform's analytical dimensions and operational efficacy.

Reintegration of Alarm and Action Plan Information: the foundation of this discussion centers on the reintegration process of alarm and action plan data into the data lake. This section delves into how the Datawizzard facilitates this reintegration, detailing the technical pathways and transformations that data undergoes to become a part of the comprehensive data repository.

Contribution to the "CHECK" and "ACT" Sub-KnowledgeMarts: the reintegrated data plays a pivotal role in enriching the "CHECK" and "ACT" segments of the KnowledgeMart. This subsection examines the utilization of alarm information within the "CHECK" segment for monitoring and evaluation purposes, and how action plan data enhances the "ACT" segment, supporting the implementation and execution of strategic initiatives.

Operational Mechanics of Datawizzard Integration: central to the effectiveness of this reintegration process is the operational functionality of the Datawizzard tool. This part of the chapter explores the capabilities of the Datawizzard in processing and categorizing alarm and action plan data for reintegration, highlighting the tool's significance in maintaining the data lake's relevance and utility.

Implications for Analytical Capabilities and Operational Execution: the reintegration of alarm and action plan data into the data lake, and its subsequent contribution to the "CHECK" and "ACT" segments, significantly impacts the platform's analytical and operational execution capabilities. This section reflects on the broader implications of this process, considering how enriched data supports the platform's ability to monitor, evaluate, and act upon strategic and operational insights.

The reintroduction of alarm and action plan data into the data lake via Aitek's Datawizzard represents a crucial mechanism for enhancing the platform's data repository and, by extension, its KnowledgeMart segments "CHECK" and "ACT." By providing a comprehensive examination of this reintegration process and its contributions to the platform's analytical and operational frameworks, this chapter highlights the importance of alarm and action plan information in the broader context of data-driven decision-making and strategic operational management within the platform.

PLANNING

This chapter investigates a critical interface within the platform that provides visibility into resources (IoT devices, human personnel, software programs, etc.) that are either currently engaged or scheduled to be utilized in the instantiation of action plans. This interface is adeptly designed to display this information through various project management tools such as an agenda, PERT (Program Evaluation and Review Technique) charts, and Gantt charts. The exploration here aims to dissect the operational framework and strategic utility of this interface, emphasizing its role in resource management, planning efficiency, and the execution of action plans within the platform's ecosystem.

Overview of Resource Visualization Interface: at the forefront of this interface's functionality is its capacity to offer a comprehensive view of all resources allocated to action plans. This section delves into the interface's design principles, focusing on how it integrates and presents data across agendas, PERT charts, and Gantt charts to facilitate detailed resource management and scheduling.

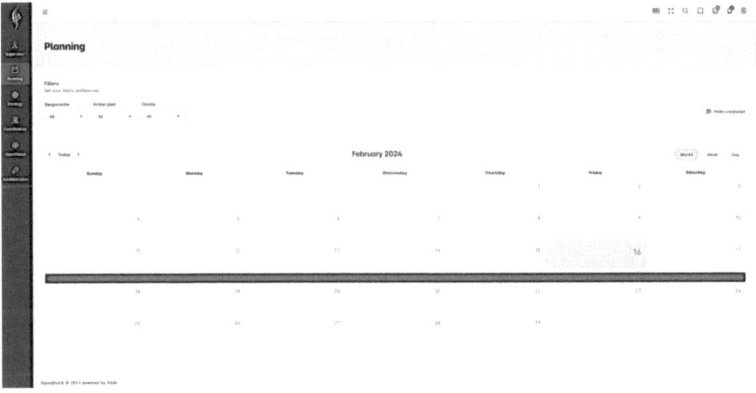

Agenda-Based Resource Management: the agenda component of the interface provides a chronological view of resource allocation, enabling users to track the deployment of resources over time. This subsection examines the agenda's role in day-to-day resource planning and coordination, highlighting its utility in ensuring that resources are effectively utilized and action plans are timely executed.

PERT Charts for Project Evaluation and Review: the inclusion of PERT charts within the interface allows for the evaluation of project timelines, identifying critical paths and potential bottlenecks in action plan implementation. This part of the chapter explores the application of PERT charts in analyzing the sequential and parallel activities involved in action plans, facilitating strategic adjustments to resource allocation and timelines.

Gantt Charts for Detailed Scheduling and Monitoring: Gantt charts offer a visual representation of action plan schedules, juxtaposing planned versus actual timelines and resource commitments. This section delves into the Gantt chart's functionality, detailing how it supports detailed project scheduling, progress monitoring, and the management of dependencies between tasks and resources.

Implications for Planning Efficiency and Action Plan Execution: the integration of these project management tools into a single interface significantly enhances the platform's planning efficiency and the effectiveness of action plan execution. This section reflects on the broader implications of this interface for the platform's operational strategy, particularly in terms of improving resource utilization, facilitating preemptive problem-solving, and enhancing overall project management capabilities.

The resource visualization interface, with its sophisticated integration of agendas, PERT, and Gantt charts, stands as a testament to the platform's advanced approach to resource management and action plan execution. By providing users with a multi-faceted view of resource allocation and scheduling, the interface plays a pivotal role in enhancing the platform's efficiency and effectiveness in operational planning and execution. This chapter has provided a comprehensive exploration of the interface's design, functionality, and strategic importance, underscoring its value in the broader context of the platform's resource management and project execution strategies.

we highlight the pivotal role of planning information in enriching the data lake, specifically through the integration facilitated by Aitek's Datawizzard tool. This process of re-injecting planning data into the data lake serves as the foundational material for the KnowledgeMart's "PLAN" segment. This chapter aims to elucidate the mechanisms through which planning information is transformed and integrated into the data lake, emphasizing the significance of this data in enhancing the platform's analytical capabilities and strategic planning processes.

The Role of Planning Information in the Data Lake: the initial focus is on understanding the value of planning information as a core component of the data lake. This section delves into how such information, encompassing resource allocations, schedules, and action plan details, contributes to a comprehensive data repository, supporting the platform's broader analytical and operational framework.

Integration Process via Datawizzard: central to the effective utilization of planning information is its integration into the data lake, facilitated by Aitek's Datawizzard tool. This sub-section explores the technical processes and metho-dologies employed by the Datawizzard to ingest, process, and store planning data within the data lake, ensuring its availability for subsequent analysis and planning activities.

Contribution to the Sub-KnowledgeMart "PLAN" Segment: The re-injected planning information significantly enriches the Sub-KnowledgeMart's "PLAN" segment, providing a rich dataset for analysis and strategic decision-making. This part of the chapter examines how the planning data is utilized within the "PLAN" segment, detailing its impact on enhancing the platform's planning accuracy, strategic foresight, and opera-tional efficiency.

Implications for Analytical Capabilities and Strategic Planning: the integration of planning information into the data lake, and its subsequent utilization within the Sub-KnowledgeMart "PLAN" segment, has profound implications for the platform's analytical capabilities and strategic planning processes. This section reflects on the broader impact of this integration, considering how enriched planning data supports more infor-med decision-making, facilitates comprehensive scenario ana-lysis, and enhances the platform's ability to plan and execute strategic initiatives effectively.

The process of re-injecting planning information into the data lake, facilitated by Aitek's Datawizzard, represents a critical mechanism for enhancing the platform's data repository and, by extension, its analytical and strategic planning capabilities. By providing a detailed examination of this integration process and its contribution to the Sub-KnowledgeMart "PLAN" segment, this chapter underscores the importance of planning information in the broader context of data-driven decision-making and strategic operational management within the platform.

Chapter 1.7: Homeland in Aitek: Performance

"Constant vigilance in performance is the sentinel's lamp, illuminating the path to unbreachable security"

In this segment of the thesis, we examine the performance and risk assessment component within the platform, particularly focusing on the performance gauge system. This graphical representation, aligned with the Aitek model, primarily derives from percentile calculations conducted within the Knowledgemart. These calculations incorporate a "group by" function that segments data by business key and time series. The results are then integrated into the FlowMarts and uploaded to a dedicated repository within the knowledge instance of the Aitek platform. This chapter aims to elucidate the methodology behind the performance gauge system, its integration with the Aitek model, and the implications of utilizing percentile-based calculations for performance and risk assessment.

Foundations of the Performance Gauge System: at the core of the platform's performance and risk assessment is the performance gauge system, a graphical tool that visualizes data analytics outcomes. This section delves into the design principles of the performance gauge, exploring how it visualizes complex data sets in an intuitive manner, facilitating easier interpretation and decision-making.

Percentile Calculations within the KnowledgeMart: the backbone of the performance gauge's data source is the percentile calculations conducted within the KnowledgeMart. This subsection examines the technical approach to these calculations, detailing the significance of the "group by" functionality that organizes data by business key and time series, enhancing the granularity and relevance of the analytics.

Integration with FlowMarts and Repository Upload: the processed data, once compiled into the FlowMarts, is subsequently uploaded to a dedicated repository within the knowledge instance of the Aitek platform. This part of the chapter explores the mechanisms of data flow from the KnowledgeMart through the FlowMarts to the repository, emphasizing the operational and strategic benefits of this structured data management approach.

Implications for Performance and Risk Assessment: the utilization of percentile-based calculations and their graphical representation via the performance gauge system significantly impacts the platform's ability to assess performance and risk accurately. This section reflects on the broader implications of this approach, considering how it supports strategic planning, operational efficiency, and risk mitigation efforts within the platform's ecosystem.

The performance gauge system, underpinned by percentile calculations and integrated within the Aitek model, represents a sophisticated approach to performance and risk assessment within the platform. By offering a detailed examination of the system's methodology, data integration process, and its significance in strategic and operational analysis, this chapter highlights the value of the performance gauge in enhancing the platform's analytical capabilities and decision-making processes.

STRATEGIC PERFORMANCE

We delve into the historical evolution and functionality of a key interface within the Aitek platform, which, since its inception in Aitek 2 (BI++), has served as a foundational element for performance monitoring and dashboard management. Despite its age and the vintage GUI of its era, this interface has experienced minimal functional evolution in terms of performance and dashboard features. Structured according to the Aitek model, the FlowMart aggregates performance at each node, facilitating a comprehensive traversal of the performance and risk tree as defined by the Aitek model through the KnowledgeBuilder. Moreover, the architecture of the document management system aligns with this logical structure, enabling the storage of documents at each node, including Mission, Business Unit, Profession, Program, Objective, and Activity. This section aims to elucidate the operational framework of this interface, highlighting its enduring relevance, the methodology of performance aggregation within the FlowMart, and the integration of document management following the same logical model.

Historical Context and Evolution of the Interface: initially introduced in Aitek 2 (BI++), this interface represents one of the platform's earliest forays into providing users with a graphical user interface (GUI) for performance monitoring and dashboard management. This section explores the interface's historical significance, its initial design considerations, and the extent to which it has evolved—or remained consistent—over subsequent platform iterations.

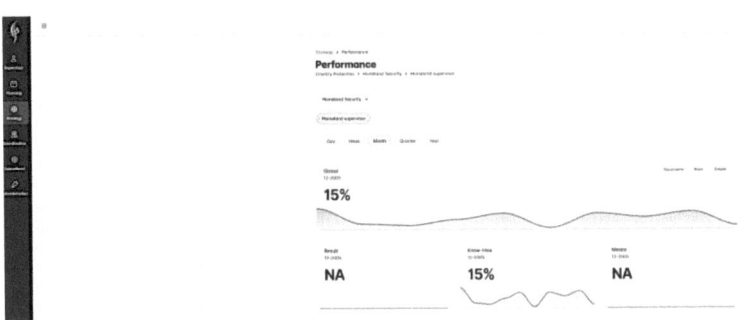

Performance Monitoring and Dashboard Management: central to the interface's functionality is its role in aggregating and displaying performance metrics across the platform's various operational nodes. This part of the chapter examines the methods for performance aggregation within the FlowMart, detailing how data is organized and visualized to support comprehensive performance and risk analysis.

Integration with the Aitek Model through KnowledgeBuilder: the interface's design and operational logic are deeply integrated with the Aitek model, as configured through the KnowledgeBuilder tool. This subsection delves into how the interface facilitates navigation through the performance and risk tree, aligning with the predefined structure of the Aitek model to enhance user engagement and analytical depth.

Document Management System Alignment: a notable feature of this interface is its document management capabilities, structured to reflect the Aitek model's logical hierarchy. This section explores the document management system's architecture, focusing on how documents can be associated with specific nodes within the model, such as Missions, Business Units, Professions, Programs, Objectives, and Activities, thereby enhancing the platform's information storage and retrieval capabilities.

OPERATIONNAL PERFORMANCE

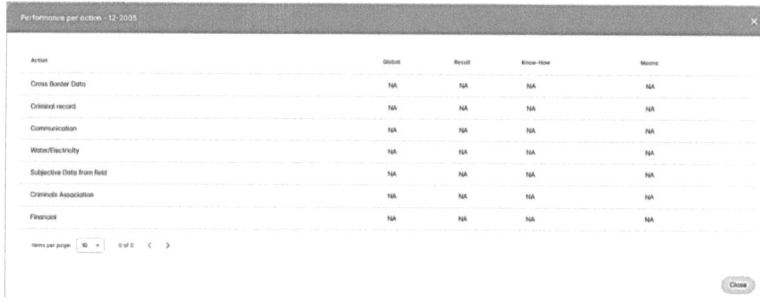

Despite its historical roots and minimal functional evolution in terms of GUI aesthetics, this interface remains a critical component of the Aitek platform, offering robust performance monitoring, dashboard management, and document storage functionalities. By providing a detailed exploration of the interface's design, functionality, and integration with the Aitek model, this chapter highlights its importance in the broader context of the platform's data analysis, performance management, and operational documentation strategies.

Chapter 1.8: Homeland in Aitek: Dashboard

"A predictive dashboard serves as a security compass, guiding through the fog of uncertainty to foresee and forestall potential perils."

In this chapter, we delve into the platform's historical reporting and dashboard interface, which exclusively utilizes FlowMart as its data source. This interface, pivotal for generating reports and dashboards, automatically calculates the distribution across various temporal granularities for each business entity. Users have the option to export data sets to Excel or PDF formats, making the interface particularly user-friendly for end-users. Furthermore, it incorporates predictive analytics capabilities through AutoML agents applied to FlowMarts, enabling future trend projections with coherence checks across higher levels of granularity. For instance, if analyzing daily data trends with a forecast extending over the next five days, the system simultaneously generates weekly predictions to ensure daily forecasts aggregate coherently on a weekly basis. Additionally, the reporting component is equipped with a configurator for lists and cross-tabulations, leveraging the JasperReport component for enhanced data presentation. This section aims to elucidate the operational framework, analytical capabilities, and user interface of the platform's reporting and dashboard feature, highlighting its significance in facilitating advanced data analysis and presentation.

DASHBOARD & REPORT

Historical Context and Data Source Integration: initially introduced as a core component for querying, this interface's reliance on FlowMart for data sourcing underscores its integral role in the platform's analytical ecosystem. This section explores the historical development of the interface and its strategic alignment with the platform's data management principles.

Automated Dashboard Calculations and Data Export: central to the interface's functionality is its ability to automatically perform calculations across temporal granularities for various business entities, coupled with flexible data export options. This subsection delves into the mechanisms supporting these calculations and the user-friendly features that enable efficient data export to Excel or PDF formats.

Predictive Analytics and Coherence Control: a distinctive feature of the interface is its predictive analytics capability, facilitated by AutoML agents that extend analytical insights into the future with a coherence check mechanism. This part of the chapter examines how the interface manages predictive analytics, ensuring that short-term forecasts align with broader temporal predictions to maintain data integrity and analytical coherence.

Operational > Dashboards

Dashboards

Amount transaction

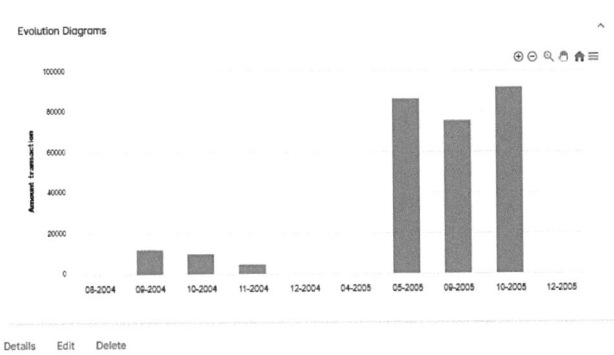

Dashboard

Reporting and Configuration Capabilities: the interface's reporting component, powered by JasperReport, offers robust configurability for generating lists and cross-tabulations. This section explores the configurational aspects of the reporting tool, highlighting how it enhances the platform's capacity for tailored report generation and sophisticated data presentation.

The reporting and dashboard interface of the platform represents a sophisticated blend of historical data integration, automated analytical calculations, predictive analytics, and configurable reporting. By providing an in-depth analysis of its design, functionality, and strategic importance, this chapter underscores the interface's role in enhancing the platform's overall data analysis and presentation capabilities, facilitating a comprehensive understanding of business trends and future projections.

Chapter 1.9: Homeland in Aitek: Supervisor Setup

"The why is the open gate to knowledge."

In the context of the Aitek platform, the supervisor serves as a critical module designed to facilitate interaction with what is termed a "knowledge cartridge." In instances where a knowledge cartridge, such as the one identified for homeland security, is pre-edited, it encompasses alarms, action plans, threats, and both manual qualitative and quantitative "order entry" inputs. These elements are already pre-configured, requiring only review and potential minor adjustments to ensure optimal alignment with the specific nuances of the local context.

However, the scenario shifts significantly when dealing with a knowledge cartridge that has been entirely customized by the end user. In such cases, the initial configuration of these parameters becomes foundational, acting as the cornerstone for the entire supervisory dynamic. This customization process is not merely a technical task but a strategic one, as it directly influences the efficacy and responsiveness of the supervisory system. It necessitates a nuanced understanding of the local environment, threats, and operational objectives to tailor the system's alert mechanisms, action protocols, and threat assessments accordingly.

This dichotomy underscores the adaptive nature of the Aitek platform, highlighting its capacity to serve both as a turnkey solution with pre-edited cartridges and as a flexible framework that can be fully customized to meet the unique demands of a client. The significance of this flexibility cannot be overstated, as it empowers users to mold the platform in ways that best support their specific operational contexts, thereby enhancing the platform's utility and effectiveness in real-world applications.

In this light, the role of the supervisor module transcends mere data processing or alert management. It becomes a dynamic interface between the platform's core capabilities and the unique informational and operational landscapes in which it is deployed. This interplay between pre-configured and fully customized knowledge cartridges illustrates the platform's versatility and the critical importance of initial parameter setting in unlocking its full potential for targeted, effective supervision.

All these elements are interconnected through an instance of knowledge, underscoring the profound significance of knowledge management within the system. This relationship is not merely operational but foundational, as the instance of knowledge serves as the bedrock upon which the system's capabilities are built and through which its functionalities are articulated.

The concept of an "instance of knowledge" in this context implies a structured aggregation of information, rules, and procedures that define how the system interprets and responds to data inputs. It is through this knowledge instance that the system gains the ability to discern between different types of threats, prioritize actions, and execute decision-making processes that are aligned with predefined objectives and strategies. The customization or pre-configuration of knowledge cartridges essentially tailors this instance of knowledge, molding it to fit the specific requirements and context of the user.

This interconnection between system objects and the knowledge instance emphasizes the critical role of intelligent design in the creation and maintenance of effective supervisory systems. It highlights the necessity for a deep understanding of the operational domain, as well as the importance of a strategic approach to knowledge management. By effectively harnessing and structuring knowledge within the system, users can ensure that the supervisory module operates not just as a reactive tool, but as a proactive entity capable of anticipating challenges and optimizing responses in real-time.

Furthermore, this interconnectedness facilitates a dynamic and iterative learning process within the system. As the knowledge instance evolves – through updates, adaptations, and refinements – so too does the system's capacity for nuanced understanding and sophisticated decision-making. This evolution underscores the adaptive nature of the platform, enabling it to remain relevant and effective in the face of changing operational landscapes and emerging threats.

In essence, the linkage of system elements to an instance of knowledge encapsulates the essence of intelligent system design. It is a testament to the power of knowledge as the cornerstone of not just the Aitek platform, but of any advanced supervisory system seeking to navigate and mitigate complex and dynamic operational challenges.

ACTION PLAN SETTING

Within this interface, the construction of action plans takes place, with each plan consisting of phases composed of specific actions. To effectively set up these plans, it is essential to configure various parameters including the requisite user groups, the theoretical duration of each phase, and the items associated with a particular type of IoTBox. Additionally, the triggering conditions for each action phase must be precisely defined, such as initiating after a certain time period, upon a click, following the return of an agent, the detection of a file, specific values at certain locations within a file, or upon the receipt of an email with a specific subject line. All these elements are finalized at the moment of the action plan's instantiation or during its execution, which in turn updates the overall planning.

This process highlights the critical importance of detailed planning and configuration in the effective management and execution of action plans within the system. The ability to specify a wide range of triggering conditions for actions reflects the system's flexibility and adaptability to different operational contexts and requirements. It allows for the creation of highly customized and responsive action plans that can cater to the unique dynamics of each scenario.

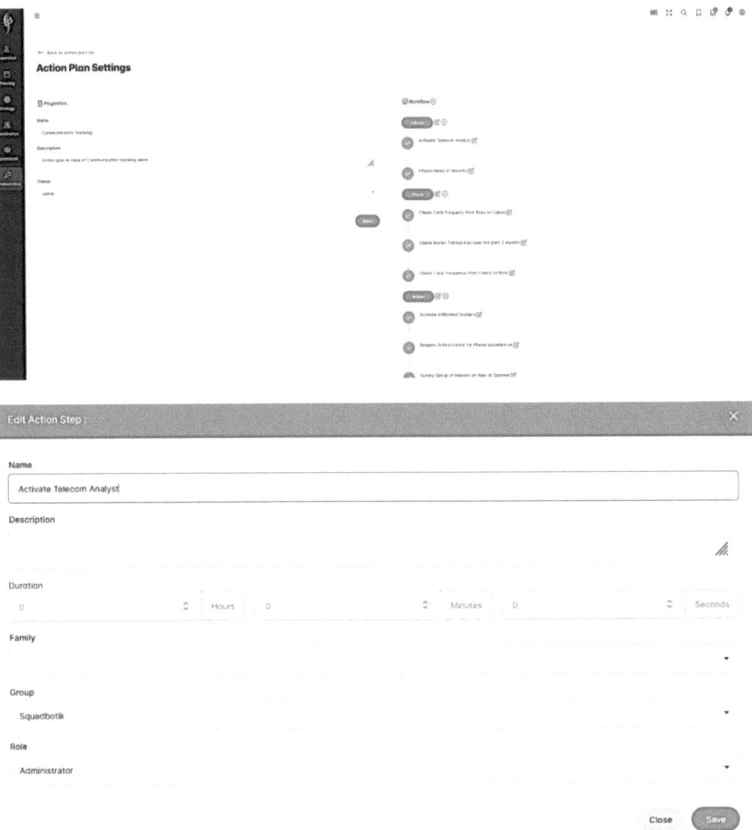

Moreover, this approach underscores the significance of integrating various types of data inputs and user interactions into the operational logic of the system. By leveraging data from IoT devices, user inputs, and external communications, the system can orchestrate complex sequences of actions that are both contextually relevant and timely. This level of integration and responsiveness is crucial for maintaining operational efficiency and effectiveness, particularly in environments where conditions can change rapidly.

Furthermore, the process of updating planning based on the action plan's execution reflects an iterative approach to operational management. It allows for the continuous refinement of action plans based on actual performance and outcomes, facilitating a cycle of improvement that can lead to enhanced operational insights and outcomes over time.

In essence, the interface for creating and managing action plans exemplifies the convergence of detailed configuration, real-time data integration, and iterative planning within the system. This integration is pivotal for achieving a high degree of operational precision and adaptability, which are essential for navigating the complexities of modern operational environments.

ALARM SETTING

In the realm of operational management and response coordination, alarms function as a critical nexus linking anomalies of all types, diagnostics/risk assessments, and the initiation of actions through the action plan system. These alarms are invariably tied to a master action plan and can be triggered through manual input, automatically by an agent, or, in some cases, ignored. Depending on the source of the alarm, it is displayed within the monitoring group's panel, ensuring that alarms related to specific anomalies or activities are assigned to the responsible group. This assignment mandates that the group organizes their duty rotations and follows a predefined knowledge model for response.

For instance, alarms arising from anomalies in an activity tied to a specific objective are allocated to the designated responsible group. This allocation process is informed by a knowledge model which dictates the response protocol. For example, an anomaly detected in the "Communication" activity of the "population and risk monitoring" objective within the "citizen protection" program would be assigned to the "Telco Expert" group. This group bears the responsibility for addressing anomalies as defined by the knowledge model, under the professional domain of "Homeland supervisor" for the "goods and people security" unit within the "country protection" mission.

≡

← Back to alarm configuration list

Alarm Configuration

🗒 Properties

Code

1

Name

Communication Tracking

Description

Suspicious communication activity

Level

HIGH

Action Plan

Communication Tracking

If an alarm is triggered by a cluster, it is directed to the group overseeing that cluster. The arrival or departure of a cluster member after calculation also triggers an alarm on "cluster". In the event of an alarm emanating from a sub-cluster within a specific geographic zone, the alarm is assigned to the group responsible for both the cluster and the zone. In cases where the alarm originates from an IoT box associated with a specific cluster and zone, the assignment follows suit. For manually triggered alarms, the group is manually assigned at the moment of alarm generation.

This systematic approach to alarm management underscores the sophistication and granularity of operational response systems. It reflects a highly structured and nuanced strategy for ensuring that every alarm, regardless of its origin, is addressed by the most appropriate and capable group. This strategy is predicated on a deep integration of operational knowledge, enabling a tailored and efficient response to a wide array of potential anomalies and risks.

Moreover, the delineation of responsibility among different groups based on the nature of the alarm and its associated activities, objectives, and overarching programs illustrates the complexity and interconnectivity of modern operational environments. It highlights the importance of a well-organized, knowledge-driven response framework that can adapt to the specific needs of each situation. Through such a framework, organizations can enhance their readiness and effectiveness in managing incidents, ultimately contributing to the safety and security of the populations and infrastructures they are tasked.

THREAT MANAGEMENT (MANUAL)

In the domain of operational analysis and response management, diagnostics are conceived as a comprehensive assessment of performance metrics within specific temporal granularities. This evaluation can focus on the intrinsic value of a metric, such as the financial risk associated with a cluster, which might be quantified at 40% for a given week, with a 15% outlier rate indicating anomalies. Based on the degree of similarity to predetermined conditions, this could trigger the activation of a corrective action plan if the similarity is substantial and closely aligns with the model's parameters. Conversely, a preventive action plan might be initiated if there is recognizable similarity, albeit not a direct match, indicating a nuanced approach to managing potential risks and anomalies.

This diagnostic process can also extend to variations in operational metrics, exemplified by a significant increase in communication volume among members, which might surge by 50% within a 24-hour period. Such a metric not only indicates a change in operational tempo but also necessitates a nuanced understanding of its implications. It requires an analytical framework that can interpret these variations within the broader context of operational health and risk management.

In crafting a response to these diagnostics, it is essential to integrate a multidimensional analysis that considers both the immediate data and its broader implications. This involves a synthesis of quantitative data, such as financial risk percentages or communication volume increases, with qualitative assessments of their potential impact on operational integrity and security. By employing a tailored action plan, whether corrective or preventive, the response mechanism becomes a dynamic tool capable of adapting to the evolving operational landscape.

The decision to trigger a specific action plan is predicated on a detailed comparison against established thresholds and patterns. This comparison is not merely numerical but involves a deep understanding of the operational ecosystem, including the potential cascading effects of anomalies and the strategic importance of maintaining operational continuity. In this context, the action plans are not static protocols but adaptive strategies informed by real-time data and historical insights.

This approach underscores the sophistication required in modern operational management, where data-driven diagnostics are complemented by strategic foresight and adaptive response strategies. It highlights the necessity for a proactive and nuanced understanding of operational dynamics, where decision-makers are equipped with the analytical tools and strategic frameworks to effectively mitigate risks and capitalize on opportunities in a timely manner. Through this lens, diagnostics become a pivotal component of a broader operational intelligence system, enabling a cohesive and resilient response to the complexities of contemporary operational environments.

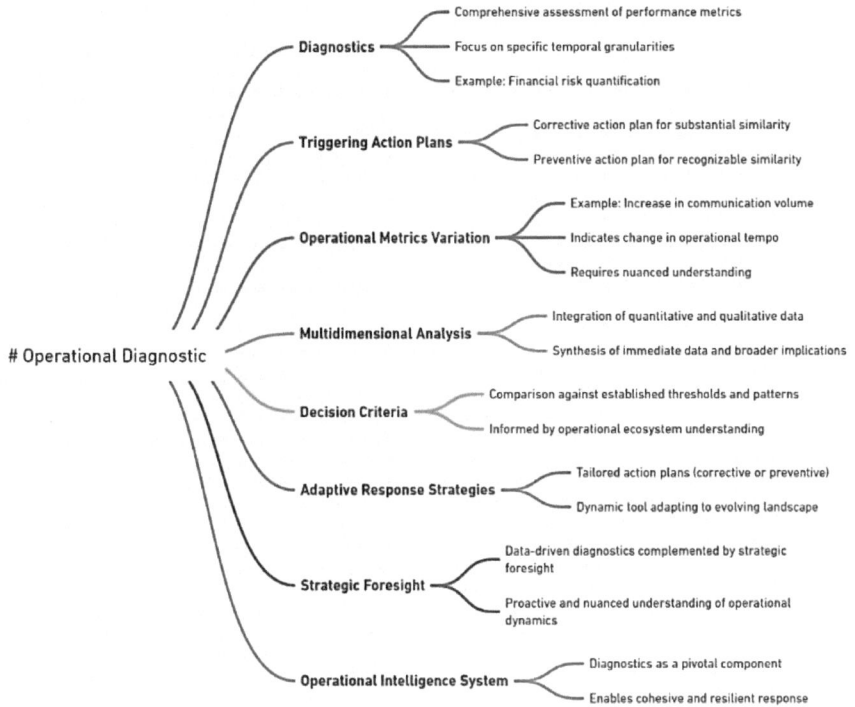

QUESTIONNAIRE BUILDING

In the context of data management and integration within complex systems, the user interface in question serves as a critical point for the creation of manual entries, whether qualitative or quantitative. This process facilitates the generation of 'order entries' that are subsequently stored in a dedicated repository. This repository, by design, functions as an extension of the data lake, expanding its utility and enhancing its capacity for data analysis and retrieval.

The significance of this interface cannot be understated. It represents a pivotal mechanism for incorporating human insights and observations into the broader data ecosystem. By enabling the manual input of data, the system acknowledges the value of nuanced, context-specific information that automated processes might overlook. This blend of qualitative and quantitative inputs enriches the data lake, providing a more comprehensive foundation for analysis and decision-making.

Questionnaire

Properties

Name
Manual Entry

Description

Response time (s)
120

Objective
Population Risk Monitoring

Criminal record
☑ Number of agent for justice

Cross Border Data
☑ Number of border police agent

Financial
☑ Budget dedicated to economic crime

The process of transforming manual entries into order entries within a dedicated repository illustrates a sophisticated approach to data management. It ensures that these inputs are not only captured but are also structured in a manner that facilitates their integration with existing datasets. This structuring is essential for maintaining the integrity and utility of the data lake, allowing for seamless querying and analysis across a diverse array of data types and sources.

Furthermore, the extension of the data lake through this method underscores the adaptive nature of modern data architectures. It exemplifies a system designed to evolve and expand, accommodating new types of data and sources of information. This flexibility is crucial in an era where the velocity, variety, and volume of data continue to escalate.

In essence, the interface acts as a bridge between the tacit knowledge held by individuals and the vast, algorithmically navigable expanse of the data lake. It encapsulates a methodology that values both the precision of quantitative data and the depth of qualitative insights. This approach not only enhances the data lake's richness but also its relevance, ensuring that it remains a vital resource for insights and intelligence in an increasingly data-driven world.

The strategic inclusion of a dedicated repository for these manual entries further exemplifies a thoughtful approach to data governance and architecture. It ensures that these entries are accessible and actionable within the larger data ecosystem, while also preserving the organizational and contextual nuances that give them value. This integration strategy embodies a forward-thinking approach to data management, where the goal is not merely to collect and store data but to weave it into a coherent, dynamic fabric of actionable intelligence.

Chapter 1.10: Homeland Security +

"In the digital age, the pen and pixel wield more power than the sword."

The challenge with media platforms is that not all operate with benign intentions; a subset is subversive, manipulating communities by exploiting vulnerabilities or inciting conflicts among groups. These actions, characterized by subversion, defamation, and encouragement of malevolent and violent acts, are ostensibly carried out under the guise of promoting democracy, religious freedom, or political liberty. However, these purported aims often serve merely as pretexts for undermining societal cohesion from within. This paper aims to dissect the mechanisms through which media can become a tool for such subversive activities, analyzing the impact on social structures and proposing strategies for mitigating these influences. By examining case studies and drawing on theoretical frameworks, we seek to understand the dynamics at play and the role of regulatory and counter-measures in preserving the integrity of public discourse and social harmony

There exists an array of vectors for information dissemination, spanning both digital and analog domains, including television and radio channels with sometimes very limited reach, blogs, and newspapers. Not to mention the prevalence of YouTube channels, TikTok, WhatsApp, Telegram, and Signal groups, Facebook pages and Messenger groups, and Twitch streams. Mobilizing sufficient resources to monitor and analyze the vast amount of content distributed across these platforms is an insurmountable task for traditional methods. This is where Artificial Intelligence (AI) steps in, offering scalable solutions to efficiently process, analyze, and interpret the data generated across these diverse media channels. AI's capability to sift through vast datasets, identify patterns, and predict potential subversive activities makes it an invaluable tool in managing the challenges posed by the multifaceted media landscape. Through machine learning algorithms and natural language processing, AI can automate the detection of harmful content, thereby supporting efforts to maintain societal stability and prevent the spread of disinformation.

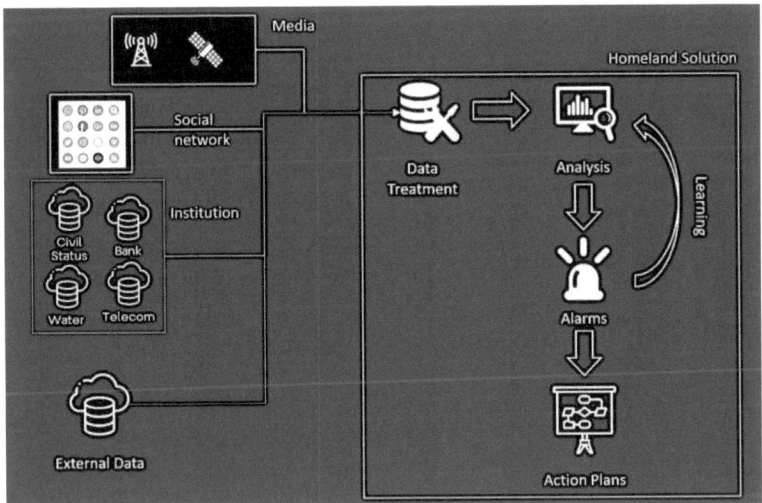

In the realm of homeland security, the integration of IoT devices and artificial intelligence (AI) significantly enhances the ability to monitor and respond to potential threats. Our approach involves deploying two distinct types of IoT boxes that serve as advanced surveillance tools, each tailored to a specific aspect of media and communication.

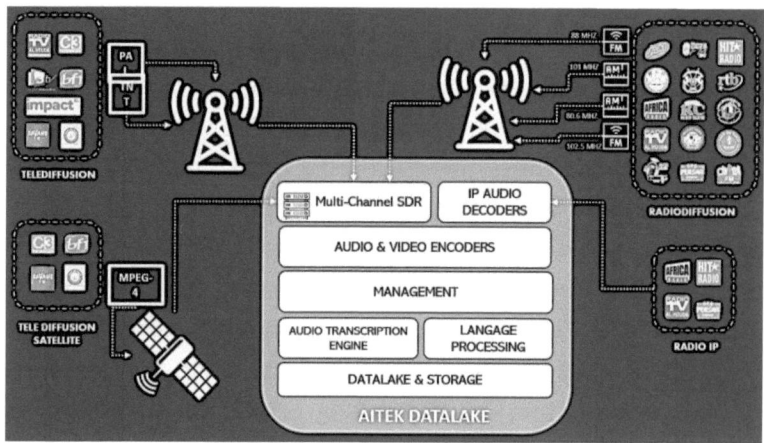

Media-Specific IoT Box: this device is engineered to scrutinize traditional media outlets, such as television and radio broadcasts, as well as print media like newspapers and journals. Utilizing cutting-edge voice and image recognition technologies, it can automatically scan and transcribe audiovisual and printed content into digital text.

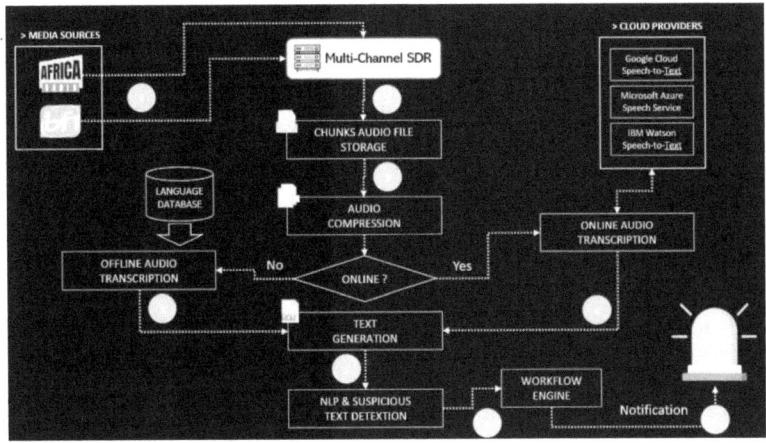

This transcription is then annotated to highlight sections that may pose a risk, based on predefined criteria related to security threats. For instance, if a particular broadcast segment or newspaper article contains language that could incite violence or is identified as spreading misinformation, the system flags this content. Each piece of flagged content is timestamped or referenced by page and paragraph for easy retrieval and review.

Social Media-Specific IoT Box: parallel to the media-specific device, this IoT box focuses on the vast landscape of digital and social media platforms, including Facebook, Telegram, Signal, TikTok, and others. It's designed to monitor and analyze the content shared across these networks, identifying and flagging posts, videos, or messages that could indicate subversive activities or the spread of harmful propaganda. By linking each social media channel to its corresponding cluster within the vector database, the system not only tracks the content but also profiles and monitors the behavior of its members. This dual-layered analysis helps in identifying not just isolated pieces of concerning content but also patterns of behavior across different platforms that could signify coordinated efforts to undermine security.

Integration with Aitek Supervisor: the alarms generated by both IoT boxes are directly communicated to the Aitek supervisor, a central AI-driven monitoring system. This supervisor assesses the risk associated with the flagged content, categorizing each alarm based on its potential threat level. It then archives the raw information alongside the text transcription, ensuring that original evidence is preserved for forensic analysis or future reference. Additionally, the super-visor can initiate predefined response protocols, ranging from closer monitoring of certain individuals or groups to alerting law enforcement agencies for further investigation.

The interconnectedness of these IoT devices with the Aitek supervisor and the vector database creates a comprehensive surveillance ecosystem. This system is capable of not just passive monitoring but proactive risk management, effectively utilizing AI to sift through the enormous volume of information generated daily across various media and social platforms. By automating the detection and analysis process, it significantly reduces the need for human resources to monitor each channel individually, enabling a more efficient and focused approach to homeland security.

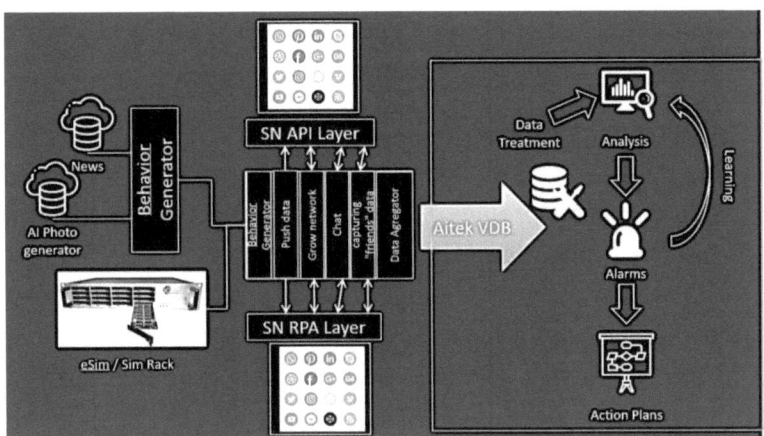

The strategy involves deploying an array of AI agents, each assigned a telephone number and a digital identity. This identity is crafted with profiles on Facebook, LinkedIn, and ac-counts on WhatsApp, Telegram, Botim, Skype, Signal, Switch, and TikTok. Through a combination of API utilization and Ro-botic Process Automation (RPA), these agents are activated and engage within specific domains.

Specialization of AI Agents: each AI agent is tailored to focus on a particular region and type of cluster, which dictates its behavior and vocabulary during interactions. This specialization allows for a nuanced approach to monitoring and analysis, ensuring that the AI can blend in and interact effectively within its designated community.

Transcription and Annotation of Communications: the activities and communications of these AI agents, including Facebook posts and WhatsApp group interactions, are transcribed into text. This textual data is then annotated based on identified risks, contributing to a rich, detailed profile of each individual within the network.

Enrichment of Individual Profiles: the information collected by the AI agents enriches the digital profiles of individuals in the database, providing a comprehensive view of their online behavior, affiliations, and potential security risks. This process allows for the dynamic updating of profiles based on new interactions and information, ensuring that the security apparatus is always informed of the latest developments within targeted clusters.

Implementation and Impact: this approach allows for a sophisticated, covert surveillance mechanism that can penetrate various social groups and networks, gathering intelligence on potential threats and subversive activities. By leveraging AI in this manner, homeland security efforts can be significantly enhanced, offering a proactive stance against internal and external threats. The utilization of AI agents across diverse platforms also ensures broad coverage of the digital landscape, making it more difficult for malicious actors to operate undetected.

Ethical Considerations: while the deployment of AI agents for security purposes offers substantial benefits, it also raises ethical considerations regarding privacy and the potential for misuse. It is crucial that such operations are conducted within the bounds of the law and with respect for individual rights, ensuring that the balance between security and freedom is maintained.

Chapter 1.11: Homeland Security ++

"In the sky's watchful eye, drones soar, turning the unseen into seen and making security not just a presence, but a guarantee"

In the realm of security and emergency management, leveraging artificial intelligence (AI) to pilot drones presents a transformative approach to monitoring and responding to situations involving potentially hostile individuals or groups. A critical application of this technology involves the precise localization of vehicles associated with such entities. The objective is to avoid the deployment of conspicuous police forces, which can inadvertently escalate tensions among the civilian population.

Furthermore, in scenarios requiring crowd management or evacuation, visibility and control are paramount. Traditional methods often fall short in efficiently overseeing such situations, particularly in the aftermath of urban incidents where navigating through congested streets becomes a challenge. Rapid deployment of medical supplies or emergency personnel directly to the operation's epicenter is crucial for effective response.

AI technology, particularly the Aitek platform and its supervisory capabilities, introduces a strategic advantage in these scenarios. Through autonomous drone piloting, Aitek's AI can optimally manage tasks such as surveillance, crowd control, and logistical support in emergency situations. By integrating advanced pattern recognition and real-time data analysis, these drones can navigate and adapt to evolving circumstances with minimal human intervention. This approach not only enhances the efficiency of emergency responses but also minimizes risks to both the responders and the general public.

The implementation of AI-driven drones in security operations underscores a shift towards more agile, discreet, and effective management of potential threats and emergency situations. This innovation stands as a testament to the potential of AI in augmenting human capabilities and redefining traditional security and emergency response paradigms.

In the context of enhancing homeland security measures, the Aitek platform, through its Homeland++ knowledge cartridge, incorporates a sophisticated 'Find Vehicle' feature accessible via the Query 360 interface of the Aitek supervisor. This functionality initiates a comprehensive action plan triggered by the input of license plate information associated with a designated target or their close associates. Users have the flexibility to manually input a full or partial, even inaccurately recorded, license plate number. Upon activation, the system strategically deploys the nearest drone container based on the latest geolocation data of the target or their associates.

The deployed drones are equipped with advanced recognition technology capable of reading and identifying license plates. Upon successful detection of a vehicle matching the input criteria, the drone locks onto the vehicle, transmitting real-time data, including its location, to the nearest police station. This process is meticulously recorded in the action plan section of the Aitek supervisor, ensuring a seamless chain of custody of information until the suspect's apprehension.

Moreover, these drones are designed for high efficiency and autonomy. After completing their mission, they autonomously return to their base for recharging. Should the operation require extended surveillance, another drone can take over the mission from the exact point of handover thanks to Aitek's integrated knowledge sharing and communication system. This seamless transition ensures continuous monitoring and tracking capabilities, significantly enhancing the operational effectiveness of law enforcement in real-time situational awareness and suspect apprehension, thereby contributing to the overall safety and security of the homeland.

In the realm of emergency response and forensic analysis, drones present a transformative solution, offering rapid, risk-mitigated transportation of samples, traces, or immediate evidence to designated analysis or investigation sites. This paper explores the multifaceted advantages of deploying drones in scenarios where access to risk-prone areas is hindered, such as post-terrorist attacks or during large cultural or sporting events. The utilization of drones not only accelerates the delivery process, thereby reducing the time frame for critical investigative activities, but also minimizes the risks of sample deterioration or loss, and potentially lowers operational costs compared to traditional transportation methods.

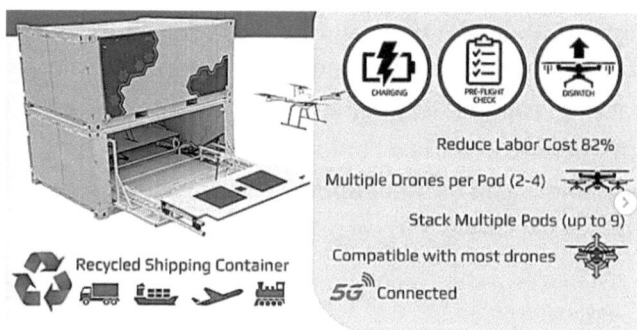

Immediately following a terrorist incident, drones can be instrumental in conducting aerial surveys to map vehicular positions around the affected zone, capturing their orientations and gathering as much information as possible about the surrounding crowd. This rapid assessment aids in the quick understanding of the scene, facilitating timely and informed responses by emergency and investigative teams. Furthermore, Hoplon's Falconet drones possess the capability to conduct interior explorations of buildings within a defined radius around the incident site. This capability is particularly invaluable for assessing structural integrity, identifying survivors or additional threats, and collecting forensic evidence without putting human lives at further risk.

This paper delves into the technological, operational, and strategic frameworks that underpin the effective integration of drone technology into emergency response and forensic investigation protocols. By examining case studies and modeling scenarios, we aim to highlight the potential of drones to revolutionize the speed, efficiency, and safety of critical operations in high-risk environments. Additionally, we propose guidelines for the ethical and legal deployment of drones in such sensitive contexts, ensuring that their use aligns with overarching principles of human rights and privacy protection.

For an effective surveillance system covering an area of 1,000 square kilometers, the deployment of approximately ten containers, each housing up to five drones, is generally required, totaling 50 surveillance-type drones. Each container is equipped with its own autonomous energy system, relying on solar power and batteries to ensure continuous operation. Furthermore, both the drones and their corresponding IoT Boxes must be registered within the Aitek engine as unique entities, adhering to the configuration parameters previously outlined.

This setup guarantees not only the sustainability and energy independence of the surveillance units but also their seamless integration into the broader security and surveillance framework provided by the Aitek platform. The registration process allows each drone and IoT Box to be precisely monitored and controlled, enhancing the efficiency of data collection and the responsiveness of the surveillance system.

The strategic placement of these containers, coupled with the advanced capabilities of the drones for real-time monitoring and data collection, forms the backbone of a highly responsive and adaptive surveillance network. This network is capable of providing comprehensive coverage over large areas, making it an invaluable asset for national security, emergency response, and environmental monitoring efforts.

In summary, the incorporation of autonomous energy solutions, along with the integration of drones and IoT technology into a centralized AI platform, represents a forward-thinking approach to modern surveillance challenges. This paper will explore the technical specifications, operational protocols, and potential applications of this innovative surveillance system, highlighting its significance in enhancing safety, security, and situational awareness across extensive geographical areas.

PART 2:
Territorial security with Aitek

"A nation's strength lies not just in its army or economy, but in the security of its borders."

Chapter 2.0: Territorial Security Concept (Aitek)

"Guard your borders as diligently as you program your AI, for both shape the safety of your realm."

Territorial surveillance represents a critical component of a nation's security apparatus, charged with the dual mandate of investigating and preempting activities within the national borders that are either directly or indirectly influenced by foreign entities and pose a tangible threat to the country's security framework. This mission mandates a multifaceted approach to safeguarding national interests, one that seamlessly integrates the realms of physical security and cyber vigilance.

The essence of territorial surveillance is rooted in its capacity to conduct continuous monitoring and sophisticated analysis of a broad spectrum of activities that could jeopardize the state's structural integrity or endanger its populace. This vigilant oversight is instrumental in identifying and mitigating risks associated with espionage, acts of sabotage, and various forms of foreign interference, all of which carry the potential to destabilize the nation's socio-political equilibrium or compromise its strategic advantages.

By extending its purview beyond mere physical threats to include cyber threats, territorial surveillance acknowledges and addresses the evolving landscape of national security threats in the digital age. The cyber dimension, characterized by its fluidity and the anonymity it affords, has become a battleground for information warfare, intellectual property theft, and infrastructure sabotage, necessitating advanced analytical capabilities and real-time monitoring systems to detect and respond to such threats effectively.

In fulfilling its mandate, territorial surveillance employs a comprehensive array of tools and technologies, ranging from satellite imagery and electronic eavesdropping to data analytics and artificial intelligence, to paint a detailed picture of potential security threats. This technological arsenal, coupled with human intelligence and strategic partnerships, enables the detection of covert operations and the imple-mentation of countermeasures to protect national interests.

Ultimately, the role of territorial surveillance in maintaining national security and sovereignty cannot be overstated. By proactively identifying and countering threats emanating from foreign powers, it ensures the preservation of the nation's stability, safeguarding its citizens, infrastructure, and strategic interests against external aggression and internal subversion.

Incorporating Autonomous Maritime and Terrestrial Beacons from an Energy Perspective with IoT Connectivity through Aitek and Supervision Integration

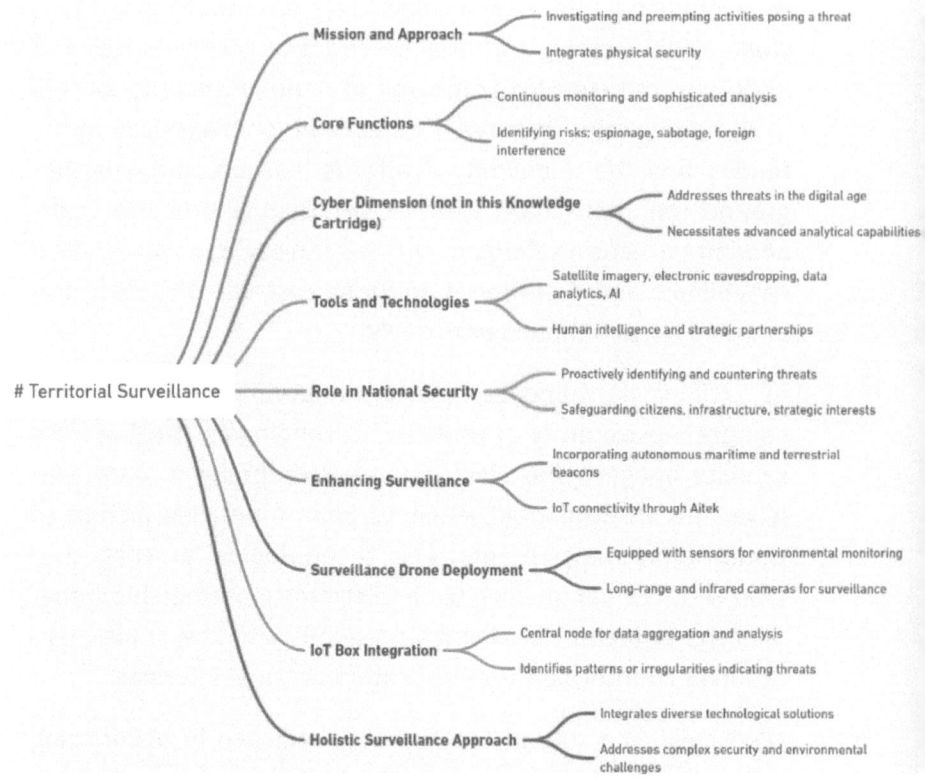

This study proposes an innovative framework for enhancing surveillance and monitoring capabilities across diverse environmental conditions by integrating autonomous maritime and terrestrial beacons. These beacons are designed with energy efficiency in mind and are interconnected through an Internet of Things (IoT) Box connected to Aitek, facilitating real-time data collection and analysis. The proposed system is further augmented by the deployment of a surveillance drone, equipped with an array of sensors including temperature, humidity, luminosity, wind, and vibration detectors, as well as long-range cameras and infrared sensors arranged in a matrix configuration. This comprehensive sensor network is aimed at providing a multidimensional understanding of environmental conditions, enhancing the capacity for early warning and response to potential threats or anomalies.

The integration of these technologies allows for the extension of territorial surveillance as described in the second part of this work, offering a scalable and adaptable approach to security and environmental monitoring. By leveraging the capabilities of autonomous beacons, drones, and a sophisticated array of sensors, the system promises to revolutionize the way territories are monitored, ensuring a higher degree of preparedness against both natural and anthropogenic challenges.

Furthermore, the use of long-range and infrared cameras in a matrix setup enables the capture of high-resolution images across vast areas, both during the day and at night, significantly improving the surveillance coverage. The IoT Box, serving as the central node for data aggregation and analysis, utilizes advanced algorithms to process the incoming data streams, enabling the identification of patterns or irregularities that may indicate emerging threats or changes in environmental conditions.

This holistic approach to territorial surveillance underscores the importance of integrating diverse technological solutions to address complex security and environmental monitoring challenges. By harnessing the power of autonomous beacons, IoT connectivity, drones, and advanced sensor technologies, the proposed framework sets a new standard for comprehensive and proactive monitoring strategies, offering significant implications for homeland security, environmental protection, and beyond.

Chapter 2.1: Territorial Security Approch (Aitek)

"Only with a good understanding of what means borders can a nation's peace be safely sheltered."

This knowledge cartridge, as part of the Aitek platform, maintains uniformity in its foundational elements and user interfaces across different modules. This consistency extends to configuration settings, alarm systems, action plans, and other operational aspects, ensuring seamless integration with the broader Aitek ecosystem.

Our primary focus lies in exploring the unique characteristics and functionalities tailored to specific industries within this knowledge cartridge.

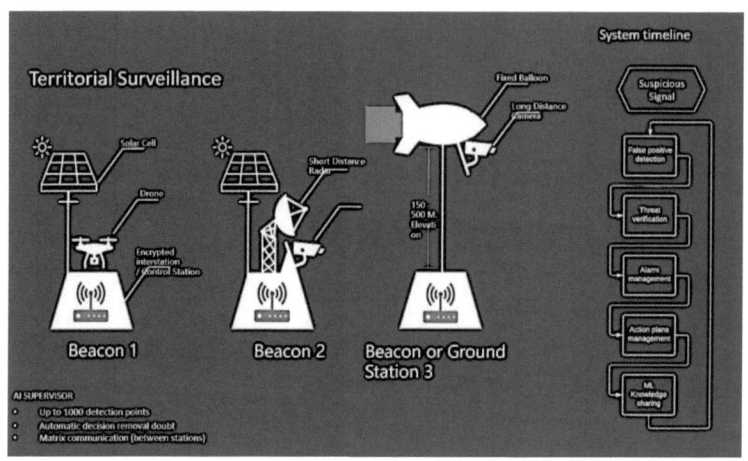

WITHIN THE REALM OF CHECKPOINT MANAGEMENT, TWO DISTINCT CATEGORIES EMERGE

Transit Points: these checkpoints serve as designated passages, whether along maritime or terrestrial routes. They may witness varying degrees of vehicular traffic, ranging from sporadic to frequent occurrences. Depending on their location and purpose, transit points might feature control mechanisms such as customs checks. The presence or absence of such control measures significantly influences operational procedures.

Restricted Access Points: unlike transit points, these checkpoints are off-limits to unauthorized personnel and vehicles. Access is strictly regulated, requiring advance notification and clearance from certified agents. Such checkpoints serve critical functions, often involving sensitive or secure areas where controlled access is paramount.

In navigating these checkpoints, a crucial consideration revolves around understanding the dynamics of the surrounding environment, particularly in relation to potential threats or hostilities emanating from "the other side." Factors such as geopolitical tensions, border security protocols, and historical contexts play pivotal roles in assessing the level of risk and determining appropriate response strategies.

By delving into the nuances of checkpoint management within this knowledge cartridge, stakeholders can gain valuable insights into optimizing operational efficiency, enhancing security protocols, and mitigating risks associated with cross-border movements and interactions.

Chapter 2.2: Territorial Security & Beacon (Aitek)

"A vigilant beacon guided by AI ensures the safety of paths yet untraveled"

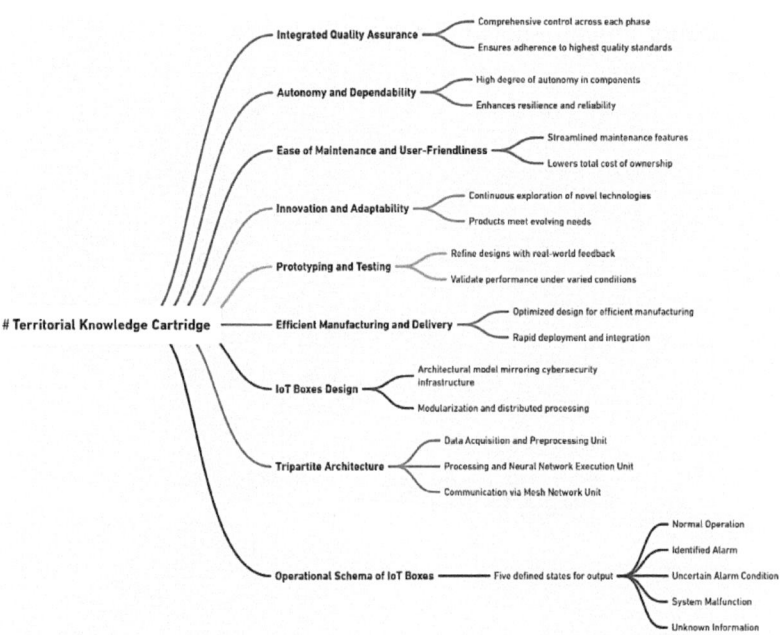

Our approach, emphasizing meticulous oversight and management across all stages of development, from conceptualization to final delivery, is designed to achieve mastery and ensure the highest standards of quality and performance for both software and hardware components. Here's a deeper look into how our strategies impact the project:

Integrated Quality Assurance: our commitment to comprehensive control across each phase ensures that every component, whether software or hardware, adheres to the highest quality standards. This relentless focus on quality minimizes risks, enhances reliability, and ensures that the final product meets our rigorous criteria, bolstering customer trust and satisfaction.

Autonomy and Dependability: in the conceptualization phase, our emphasis on imbuing components with a high degree of autonomy minimizes their dependency on external factors. This strategic foresight not only enhances the resilience and reliability of our products but also ensures they perform optimally in a wide range of operational scenarios, making them more versatile and appealing to users.

Ease of Maintenance and User-Friendliness: by integrating design features that facilitate streamlined maintenance and reduce downtime, we not only extend the lifespan of our products but also significantly lower the total cost of ownership for our users. Our focus on simplicity, without compromising on functionality, optimizes user experience by making our products more accessible and easier to use, broadening our potential market.

Innovation and Adaptability: despite our commitment to simplicity and reliability, innovation remains at the forefront of our design process. Our continuous exploration of novel technologies and methodologies enhances our products' functionality and performance. The integration of features for rapid relocation and installation underscores our products' adaptability, ensuring they meet the evolving needs of diverse environments and operational requirements.

Prototyping and Testing: our prototyping phase allows us to refine our designs based on practical, real-world feedback, ensuring that the autonomy, maintenance ease, and simplicity principles are effectively realized. Subsequent rigorous testing validates our products' performance under varied conditions, further aligning them with our high-quality standards and ensuring they meet our overarching objectives.

Efficient Manufacturing and Delivery: our design optimization ensures that the manufacturing process is both efficient and aligned with our quality standards. The focus on adaptability facilitates a smoother transition to market, enabling rapid deployment and integration into users' environments, thereby reducing the time and costs associated with installation and setup.

Our approach is a testament to our commitment to excellence, innovation, and user-centric design, ensuring that we deliver products that are not only technologically advanced but also reliable, easy to maintain, and adaptable to the needs of our users.

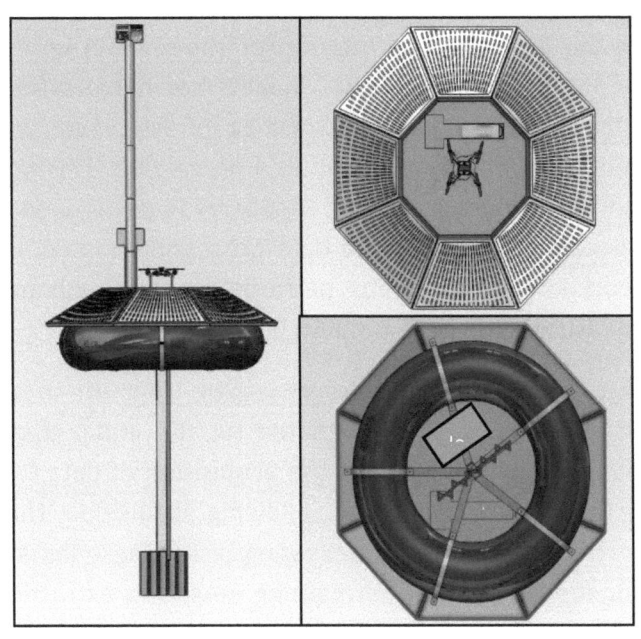

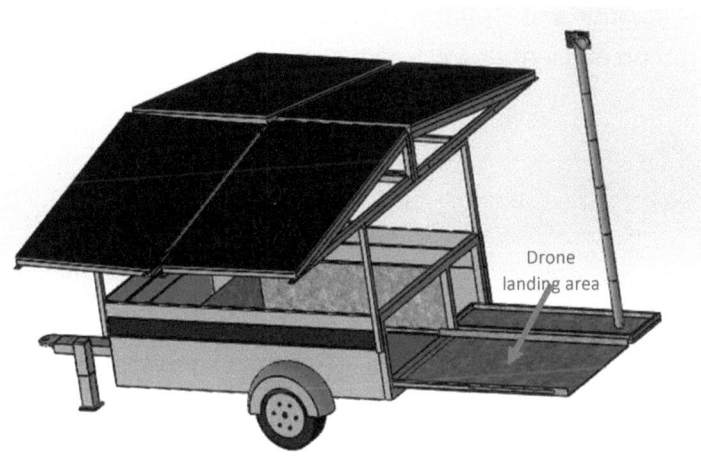

In the design of our Internet of Things (IoT) Boxes, we have adopted an architectural model that mirrors the approach utilized within our cybersecurity infrastructure, emphasizing modularization and distributed processing. This model incorporates a cluster of three Raspberry Pi devices, each assigned specific roles within the data processing and communication workflow, to optimize performance and enhance security measures. The configuration is as follows:

Data Acquisition and Preprocessing Unit: the first Raspberry Pi in the cluster is designated for the initial stages of data handling, which includes the acquisition of data from various IoT sensors and devices. Following acquisition, this unit performs preliminary preprocessing tasks. These tasks are crucial for reducing noise, normalizing data, and extracting relevant features, thereby preparing the data for more complex analysis. This preprocessing step is vital for ensuring the quality and usability of the data, facilitating more accurate and efficient downstream processing.

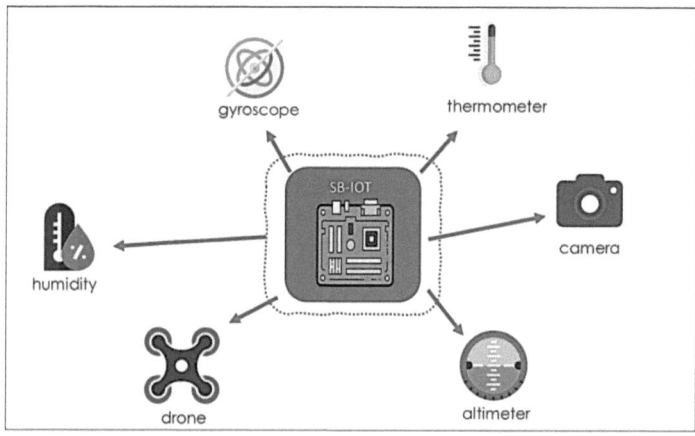

Processing and Neural Network Execution Unit: the second Raspberry Pi is responsible for the core computational tasks. This includes detailed data analysis and the execution of neural network models. Neural networks are employed to identify patterns, make predictions, or detect anomalies within the data, depending on the specific application of the IoT Box. This unit must possess a higher computational capability compared to the first, as it handles the most resource-intensive operations, including machine learning algorithms and data analytics processes.

Communication via Mesh Network Unit: the third Raspberry Pi is tasked with managing communication functions. It facilitates the transmission of processed data and insights to end-users or other systems and ensures the integration of the IoT Box within a broader network infrastructure. This unit utilizes a Mesh network for communication, chosen for its reliability and resilience. Mesh networks offer advantages such as self-healing, scalability, and efficient data routing, making them particularly suited for IoT applications where devices may be distributed across various locations.

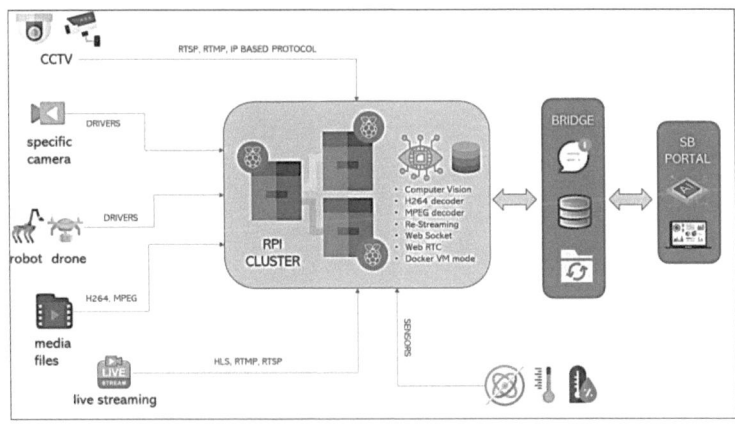

This tripartite architecture underscores our commitment to creating IoT solutions that are not only efficient and scalable but also secure and resilient. By dividing responsibilities across three specialized units, we can optimize the processing power and functionality of each Raspberry Pi, ensuring that our IoT Boxes are capable of meeting the demands of sophisticated cybersecurity and data processing tasks. This approach also enhances the system's overall reliability and performance, by enabling parallel processing and ensuring that communication is maintained even in the face of individual unit failures or network disruptions.

In the operational schema of our IoT Boxes, there are five defined states for output, each triggering specific actions to manage and respond to the data and situations encountered:

Normal Operation: when everything is functioning correctly, there is no need for immediate communication. However, key information is archived with timestamps for record-keeping and future reference. This ensures that even during periods of normal operation, valuable data is not lost but is instead stored for analysis or regulatory compliance.

Identified Alarm: upon detection of an alarm condition, the system initiates an alert protocol. This involves sending an alarm number, a photograph, and the last 10 seconds of video footage to the monitoring center. This provides immediate, actionable information to respond to the alarm, enabling quick decision-making and intervention if necessary.

Uncertain Alarm Condition: if there's uncertainty regarding an alarm, the system deploys a drone for further investigation. This step is crucial for verifying the nature of the alarm without dispatching human personnel immediately, optimizing response times and ensuring safety.

System Malfunction: in the event of a system failure, a specific protocol is activated to address and rectify the issue, maintaining the integrity and functionality of the IoT Boxes.

Unknown Information: when the system encounters unknown data or situations, it sends a photograph and the last 10 seconds of video footage to the central monitoring station. Here, a human supervisor reviews the information to determine whether it represents a genuine threat or alarm. If validated as a danger, the action plan is executed, and the neural network for that specific type of beacon is recalibrated. The updated model is then transmitted to all beacons of the same type, facilitating immediate knowledge sharing across the network.

In cases of uncertainty about an alarm, the operator can mandate a verification of the alarm condition at the beacon and reinitiate the learning process to incorporate this new knowledge into the system. This process ensures that the system is continuously learning and adapting to new situations, enhancing its accuracy and reliability over time.

Additionally, the beacons are programmed to upload their data to a data lake once every 24 hours. This daily compilation of knowledge is then re-analyzed, and a new version is disseminated across the network. This regular update cycle ensures that all beacons benefit from the latest insights and improvements, fostering a dynamic and evolving security ecosystem that enhances the overall safety and efficiency of the monitored area.

Chapter 2.3: Territorial Security & Architecture (Aitek)

"A vigilant beacon guided by AI ensures the safety of paths yet untraveled"

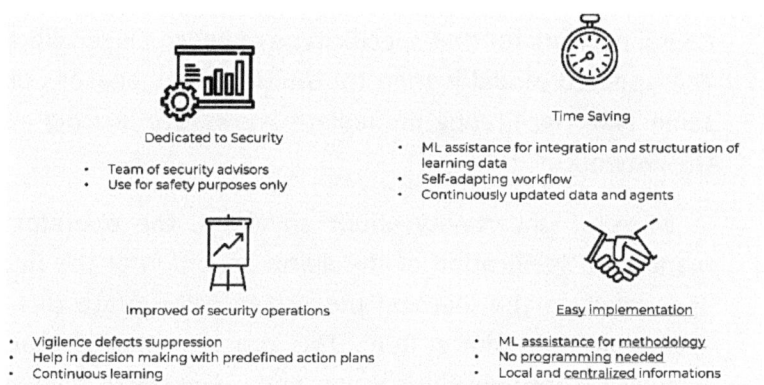

Defining geographical zones and deploying a beacon matrix along with their IoT Boxes and associated equipment (sensors, drones, etc.) forms the foundation of our system's operational setup. Here's a detailed breakdown of the process, structured to ensure the system's effectiveness from deployment through to full operational status:

Geographical Zone Definition: the initial step involves identifying and defining specific geographical zones that require monitoring. These zones are selected based on various criteria, including risk assessment, the strategic importance of the area, and specific security needs. This phase is critical for tailoring the deployment strategy to meet the unique requirements of each zone.

Deployment of Beacon Matrix with IoT Boxes: once the zones are defined, a matrix of beacons equipped with IoT Boxes is deployed across the designated areas. Each IoT Box, accompanied by the necessary sensors and drones, is strategically placed to maximize coverage and ensure comprehensive monitoring. This matrix is designed to provide a seamless flow of information, allowing for real-time data acquisition and processing.

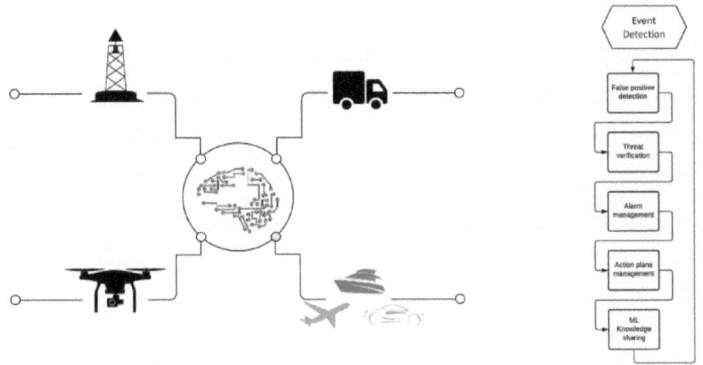

Initial Knowledge Acquisition Phase: with the system deployed, the initial phase of knowledge acquisition begins, focusing on establishing a baseline of what constitutes normality within each zone. During the first week of operation, all events are automatically flagged as normal to gather a broad dataset of typical activity. This approach allows the system to learn the regular patterns and behaviors within the zone, which is essential for distinguishing between normal and anomalous events in later stages.

Transition to Manual Validation: as the volume of unknown messages becomes manageable, the responsibility shifts to human operators to validate unknown information re-ported by the beacons. This transition marks a critical point in the system's learning process, where operator insights help refine the accuracy of event classification, ensuring that the system can reliably differentiate between normal and suspicious activities.

Entering Full Production Mode: once the operator validation process is established, and the system has been fine-tuned based on the initial learning phase, the zone enters full production mode. In this stage, the system is fully operational, with a sophisticated understanding of the normalcy baseline, allowing for real-time, accurate detection and response to security events.

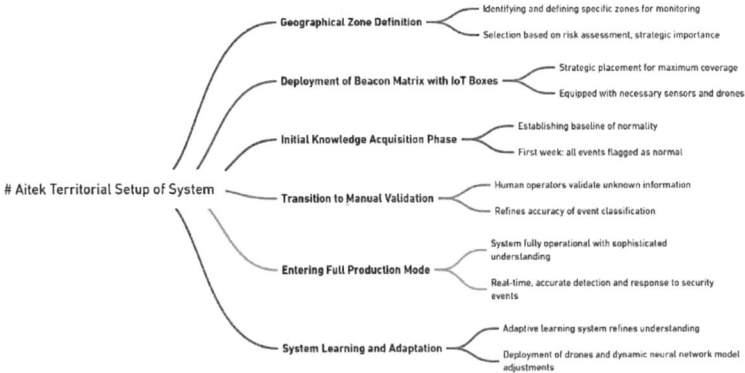

This process ensures that each zone is not only equipped with state-of-the-art monitoring technology but also benefits from an adaptive learning system that continuously refines its understanding of normal and abnormal events. The deployment of drones and the dynamic adjustment of the neural network models based on human operator feedback and automatic learning mechanisms ensure that the system remains at the cutting edge of security technology, offering unparalleled protection and situational awareness.

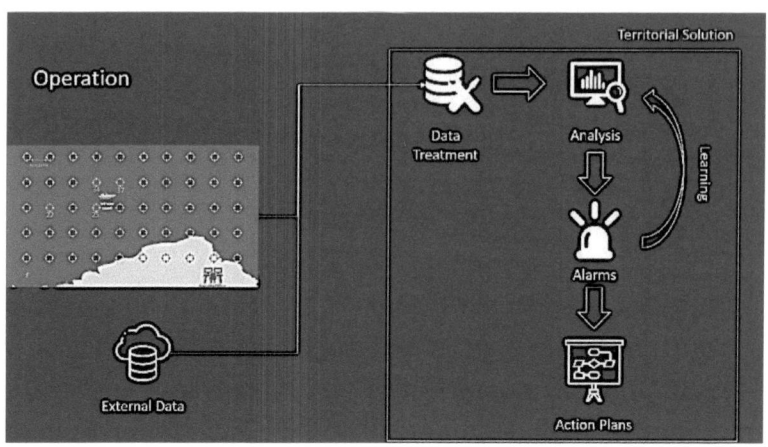

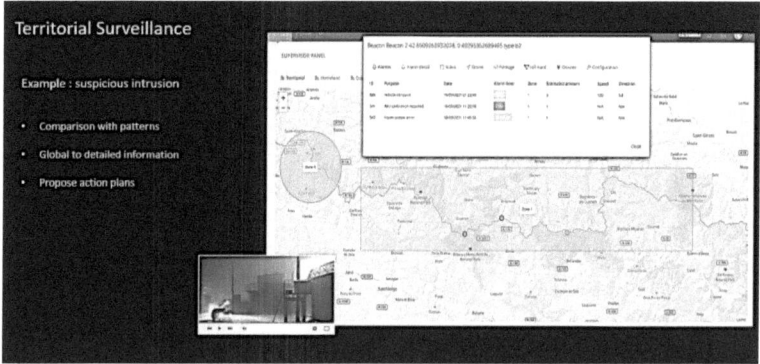

PART 3:
Knowledge cartdridge Implementation

"A vision without action is merely a dream, but vision with action can change the world."

Chapter 3.0: Aitek Plateforme Setup

"A plan well executed is more valuable than a hundred merely conceived."

The deployment of the Aitek platform encompasses a sequence of meticulously defined steps, beginning with a standard installation process executed from the root user account on a system with minimal dependencies. This systematic approach ensures the integrity and efficiency of the installation, setting a robust foundation for subsequent operations. The installation procedure culminates in the creation of a knowledge instance distinct from Aitek, alongside the configuration of users, including the assignment of a primary owner for the knowledge cartridge. This step is crucial for delineating access and administrative rights within the platform.

Following the initial setup, the process advances to align with specific recommendations for virtual machine (VM) configurations and disk specifications as provided by the cartridge publisher. This alignment is essential for optimizing the platform's performance and ensuring compatibility with the knowledge cartridge's requirements. The subsequent phase involves importing the Aitek knowledge cartridge demo version, a critical step for integrating predefined analytical capabilities and datasets into the platform.

PRE-REQUISITES FOR AITEK INSTALLATION (MINIMAL)

VM	Goal	Core	RAM	Hard Drive
VM Datalake	Datalake	8	64 Go	20 To SSD
VM Repository	Data Base Repository Aitek	8	64 Go	1 To SSD
VM VDB1	Vectorial Data Base	8	64 Go	10 To SSD
VM Front	Front Engine + Front Supervisor	8	64 Go	256 Go SSD
VM Back + IoT	Aitek Back	8	64 Go	256 Go SSD
VM Back + IoT	ML Container + IoT Listener	8	64 Go	1 To SSD

Upon successful importation of the knowledge cartridge, a series of demo tests are executed. These tests are designed to validate the platform's functionality and the cartridge's analytical prowess. The outcomes of these tests are meticulously compared against the expected results detailed in the installation manual. This comparison is not merely a procedural checkpoint but a vital assurance of the system's readiness and reliability for operational deployment. It confirms the platform's adherence to predefined operational standards and its capability to perform complex analytical tasks as in-tended.

This comprehensive approach to the installation and validation of the Aitek platform underscores the importance of thorough preparation, precise execution, and rigorous testing in establishing a reliable and effective analytical infrastructure. By adhering to these steps, organizations can ensure that their Aitek platform is optimally configured, ready to support advanced data analysis, and equipped to deliver actionable insights. This foundation is critical for leveraging the full potential of the Aitek platform in driving informed decision-making and achieving strategic objectives.

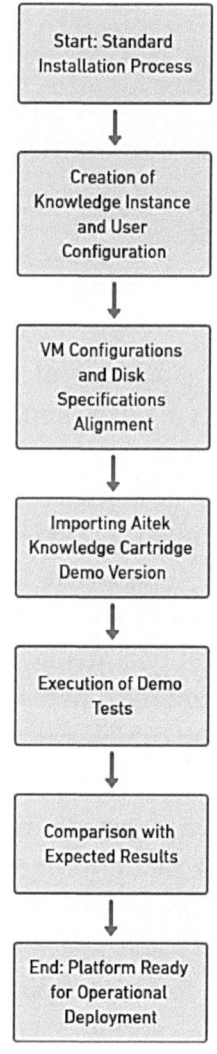

Chapter 3.1: Knowledge Cartridge Setup

"Guard your borders as diligently as you program your AI, for both shape the safety of your realm."

The process of integrating and optimizing the Aitek platform within an organizational setting involves several critical steps, each designed to ensure the platform's functionality aligns with the specific domain expertise and operational requirements of the organization. This detailed approach not only facilitates a seamless adaptation of the platform to the user's environment but also empowers users through comprehensive training and certification, ensuring they are well-equipped to leverage the platform's capabilities to their fullest potential.

Installation and Configuration: the initial phase involves the meticulous installation and configuration of the Aitek platform. This foundational step is crucial for setting up the system's infrastructure, ensuring that the platform's core functionalities are in place and operational. The creation of a knowledge instance, which serves as the platform's intellectual backbone, is closely followed by the importation of the designated knowledge cartridge. This cartridge, a repository of domain-specific expertise, is instrumental in tailoring the platform's capabilities to the user's specific needs.

License Activation and Data Importation: following the setup, the activation of the necessary licenses is critical to unlock the platform's full capabilities. The importation of a "sandbox" database provides a controlled environment for testing and experimentation, allowing users to familiarize themselves with the system's features without risking the integrity of live operational data.

Training and Certification: concurrent with the technical setup is the execution of a comprehensive training program, designed to equip users with the necessary skills and knowledge to effectively utilize the platform. This educational component is critical, as it ensures that users are not only familiar with the system's functionalities but also competent in applying them within their specific operational contexts. The certification process, which culminates in a competency examination, serves as a benchmark for proficiency, ensuring that certified users meet a standardized level of expertise.

Gap Analysis and Customization: the transition from training to practical application involves a thorough gap analysis, aimed at identifying any discrepancies between the platform's capabilities and the organization's operational needs. This analysis is pivotal in pinpointing areas that require customization or further development to fully meet the user's requirements. The identified gaps are categorized based on their nature and the feasibility of their resolution, ranging from immediate interface adjustments to the need for custom-developed solutions.

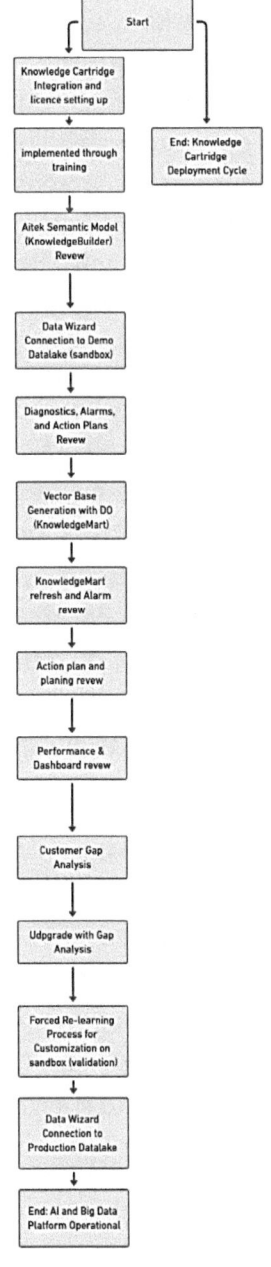

Implementation and Support: for features that can be modified through the interface, users are empowered to make these adjustments, often with the guidance and support of the platform's training personnel. This hands-on approach not only fosters a deeper understanding of the system's capabilities but also encourages a sense of ownership among users. For more complex requirements that necessitate custom solutions, the technical sales department plays a crucial role in providing tailored proposals, ensuring that the platform not only meets but exceeds the specific needs of the organization.

In the final phase of establishing a comprehensive data management and analytics framework, after the initial complete data refresh to construct the inaugural Knowledge Mart, Flow Mart, etc., a strategic evaluation of the system's architecture and performance optimization is imperative. This phase involves a series of reflective and forward-looking considerations aimed at enhancing the system's scalability, efficiency, and analytical capabilities.

Specialized Repository Creation: the development of specialized repositories on distinct virtual machines (VMs) represents a pivotal step in this process. By allocating specific repositories to dedicated VMs, the system can achieve a higher level of organizational clarity and operational efficiency. This segmentation allows for more targeted data management practices, facilitating quicker access and processing of data relevant to specific analytical tasks.

Scalability and Performance Enhancement: increasing the number and computational power of VMs dedicated to vector databases is a critical strategy for accommodating growing data volumes and complexity. This approach not only ensures the system's ability to scale in response to increased demands but also enhances its performance in handling high-dimensional data analysis, which is essential for advanced analytics and machine learning applications.

Infrastructure Optimization: separating the VMs for the Knowledge Mart from those of the replica and the Query360, and allocating distinct VMs for AI containers and IoT Box listeners, represents a strategic optimization of the infrastructure. This separation ensures that each component of the system operates within an environment tailored to its specific computational and storage needs, thereby improving overall system performance and reliability.

Refresh Strategy and Incremental Updates: following the structural and performance enhancements, a full data refresh is conducted to benchmark the system's improved capabilities. This comprehensive refresh serves as a baseline for transitioning to an incremental update model for the Knowledge Mart. By adopting an incremental approach, the system can maintain up-to-date analytical capabilities with minimal disruption, ensuring that data remains current and reflective of the latest operational realities.

This holistic approach to the final phase of system development underscores the importance of continuous evaluation and adaptation in data management and analytics infrastructure. By thoughtfully considering the allocation of resources, enhancing scalability, optimizing infrastructure, and refining data refresh strategies, organizations can create a robust and responsive analytical ecosystem. This ecosystem not only supports current analytical needs but is also well-positioned to adapt to future challenges and opportunities, thereby ensuring sustained organizational insight and decision-making capabilities.

© 2024, Edition Copernicus IP

© 2024, Bruno Ciroussel

Printed in Europe